The Smoking Section
Memories of America's Most Hated Vice

Unfiltered
Stories

Edited by Lizzy Miles

Printed in the United States of America

First Printing, 2016

ISBN: 1937574083
ISBN-13: 978-1-937574-08-6

This book is dedicated to the Kuhn brothers. I blame them for making clove cigarettes seem cool in 1985.

Contents

Acknowledgements

I want to express my deep appreciation to the authors who submitted their stories for this anthology. A special thanks to Jenn Dlugos who wrote stories, helped me recruit many of the amazing writers, and also gently nudged me a few times over the years when this project fell by the wayside. I also want to thank Julia Wagner for her editing assistance. Gratitude also to Kristin Boes, a nonsmoker, who agreed to read and provide editing suggestions.

Introduction

Despite any appearances to the contrary, this is not a pro-smoking book; neither is it an anti-smoking book. This is not a commentary on smoking in society; this book captures our *personal* love/hate relationships with cigarettes and the habit of smoking. Some of the writers hate that they love/loved smoking. Some of the writers love to hate smoking. Many stories are laugh out loud funny, and a few are serious. This is how our relationship with smoking goes. This book was a labor of love for thirteen years because I found it too hard to work on when I was trying not to smoke. Ultimately, I decided to push through to publish because I think these are really good stories and they need to be shared.

Nicotina
Alex Jones

When I was a kid my mom was a chain smoker. There were ashtrays all over the house – fancy brass ashtrays, heavy glass ashtrays, ashtrays that were abalone shells – and Mom always, always had a smoke in her hand. Unlike my younger brother, who hated it and still complains about it to this day, I never thought much about it; that was just the way things were. On the other hand, I was not curious about trying it myself.

But snuff, on the other hand ... I grew up in small-town Ohio, and nearly every guy had a ring-shaped faded patch in the back pocket of his jeans from his Skoal or Copenhagen can. One day I was riding in my older neighbor's car (a beat up Chevelle or Nova, some cool redneck muscle car) and saw he had a can of snuff in the dash. I asked him if I could have it. I don't know whether it was because he was a responsible young man or because his father was a local judge, but he said he would only give it to me with my parents' permission.

I can't remember which parent I asked, but whichever one it was surprised me by saying yes. I got that can of Happy Days snuff (don't ask me how they got away with that copyright infringement), and stuffed a wad between my cheek and gum, and ... wow, what a head rush! My first buzz! My long and tumultuous relationship with Nicotina had begun.

Long after I had switched to Copenhagen – a man's snuff – and become thoroughly addicted, my parents regretted their earlier decision and told me I had to quit. Oh, the angry teenage joy I felt in pointing out my mother's hypocrisy knew no bounds – and had no effect on the argument. I was to quit, end of story. So my habit went underground.

But this is a story about smoking, which I discovered at seventeen is much sexier to girls than a mouthful of wet tobacco, even in Ohio. I was introduced to cigarettes by a friend's girlfriend, who brought over a big box of "cocktail cigarettes," which

I think means they're fancy colors and taste terrible. Nevertheless – quicker buzz, bigger head rush! Let's do this!

And so it went, the same way it does for every smoker: I smoked when I was mad, I smoked when I was sad, I smoked when I was happy, I smoked when I was bored, and – most of all – smoked when I had a drink in the other hand. I was a smoker. It defined me, set me apart from all the sheep, made me look badass. All through my late teens and early twenties, I never gave a single thought to quitting. Why? I was invincible!

Then the year 2000 loomed on the horizon. I remembered when I was a kid and thought about how old I'd be at the turn of the millennium. Thirty! I'd be three decades old when every machine in the world suddenly forgot what it was doing! And then I felt old, and not nearly so invincible. Sort of wheezy, in fact.

So I decided to quit. And then decided to quit again. And again. Every time, I found a completely plausible rationalization for going back to Nicotina.

And every time, she opened her smelly arms wide. I knew I should quit, but … I didn't want to. I associated smoking with almost everything I ever did, and severing that connection felt like giving up some part of me. Being a non-smoker would be so boring.

Then came the not-a-tornado. I was visiting my parents in Smalltown, Ohio (I had since moved to Urbansprawl, Ohio) to see my dad act in a play, and while we were in the theater a spectacular weather event occurred. Meteorologists call it a "bow echo," but to the layman looking at the green sky and the Dumpsters hurled onto trucks, it's a tornado with no funnel cloud. It brought down hundreds of trees and nearly every power line in town, and my family was stranded, without power, without a route home, and (most importantly for me) without cigarettes.

Everything turned out okay – stumps were turned into chainsaw sculptures, roofs were replaced, and power was restored – and I had a minor epiphany: If I could make it through a not-a-tornado without a smoke, I could sure as hell make it through a regular day without one. That was the moment I did want to quit, and believed that I actually could. I failed a few more times, of course, because you know it ain't easy, but finally I tried the patch. In August of the year 2000, I had my last cigarette. And I have to say that it was one of the hardest things I have ever done, maybe my proudest achievement, and I have never once regretted it.

And – oh yeah, my chain-smoking mom? She managed to quit before I did and is now the fittest 70-year-old I have ever seen. Show off.

Alex Jones grew up in the Midwest, went to college in the Midwest, and worked for an insurance company in the Midwest for six years before thinking to himself, What the hell?? He then moved to Seattle, began working on video games, and realized that money is really only good for fantastic food and tasty cocktails.

That's How I Roll
Steve Russell

When I first arrived at college in London I blew
an entire year's student loan in three months. This
meant some serious economizing needed to be done.
Obviously, giving up cigarettes was out of the
question, so I decided to cut costs by rolling my
own. I'd tried this in the past with less than
encouraging results. These early efforts had not
been readily identifiable as cigarettes; in fact they
were not even vaguely tube-like. They would
perhaps have served as novelty paper boats but as a
mechanism for the inhalation of tobacco smoke they
were a complete failure. Still, these were desperate
times so I was willing to give it another shot. One of
the older lads in my class smoked roll-ups so I
familiarized myself with the little blocks of rolling
tobacco he used (Golden Virginia). He was
rumored to have been in prison so I assumed he was
an expert in this field.

Armed with this insider knowledge, I felt fairly cocky when I walked into the local store and asked for 25 grams of Golden Virginia, just like it said on the pack. Unfortunately, although the label may have used the metric system the storekeeper most certainly did not and he flatly refused to conduct the transaction in grams. "What do you want? An ounce, half an ounce?" he snapped impatiently. I was glad of the hint since I had absolutely no idea. I might have wanted a hundred ounces for all I knew. Since he'd given me a hint I suggested half an ounce and hurried away with my purchase.

I practiced rolling in the privacy of my dorm room. Eventually I could fashion something that could actually be smoked, although it has to be said I never managed it with any panache. They always came out too thin for a start, but since I was trying to save money this was all to the good. The trouble was I now found myself on a downward spiral of tobacco penny-pinching. Before long I was picking apart the butts in my ashtray to salvage enough tobacco to roll a 'fresh' cigarette. This is unsavory enough, but I soon went beyond this and started picking apart other people's discarded cigarette ends.

I ended up carrying around an old tobacco tin so I could squirrel away 'found' tobacco when the opportunity arose and store it for later use. This bastard mix of old flake did not keep very well and would often not pack together, so I had to develop a technique of lighting up that involved keeping the cigarette pointing sharply upwards; to do otherwise ran the risk of the fine powdery tobacco simply falling out like grains of sand.

It will be obvious at this point that there was not much glamour left in my smoking addiction. Many homeless people maintain higher standards in their smoking habits; and this was a literal truth, as I found out once while waiting to catch a train at Bromley South Station. A scruffy bearded gentleman, practically in rags and coated in grime - clearly no stranger to the streets - approached me and asked for a smoke. I shrugged and offered him my little tobacco tin, saying he was welcome to roll one for himself. He took the tin with some enthusiasm, but this enthusiasm visibly waned as he opened it and cast his eyes on the haphazard clumps and tufts of dried-out tobacco. He gave me a sorrowful look. It was a look that also contained a slight amount of embarrassment, and not a little pity. "No thanks," he muttered gently, as he handed me back the tin and shuffled away. I rolled one for myself and puffed on it contentedly, recognizing a new low but yet feeling strangely pleased with myself.

Once, quite by accident, my roll-up habit caused an expensive party to be closed down and all the guests ejected. I was paying a visit to a friend at Bristol University and we found ourselves invited to a glamorous celebration on a boat in honor of a fellow student's 21st birthday. A hundred or so guests were onboard and things were going along merrily. For some reason I started to puff on my innocent roll-up as if it were a joint. I was just horsing around but a little crowd gathered and before I knew it, I was passing it around the circle.

The power of suggestion is an amazing thing: my humble little tube of tobacco seemed to be creating an awful lot of mellow contentment. I think someone even muttered "that's some good shit, man."

Before long, this foolish nonsense attracted the attention of a tough-looking bouncer, who marched up to me just as the "joint" came back my way. He glared at me and demanded to know what I was doing. Safe in the knowledge that I was operating quite within the bounds of the law, I exaggerated my stoner pantomime yet further. I took a couple more intense tokes and with bleary eyes offered the smoke his way: "go ahead, take some yourself man."

Unfortunately he failed to see the funny side. Not only that, he refused to believe that this was not a real joint, despite my loud protestations as he threw me off the boat. I felt pretty sorry for myself as I sat alone on the dock, listening to the party carry on without me. Since I couldn't think of anything else to do, I rolled another cigarette. Before I'd finished it, I heard some sort of commotion on the boat and a voice over the loud speaker announcing something about "illicit substances" and asking everyone to leave. Sure enough, all of the guests were being thrown off the boat on account of my impulsive little prank.

I felt a bit sorry for the guest of honor, the poor birthday boy whose party was ruined. In later life he became a journalist for the BBC and I occasionally see him on television. I don't know if he ever found out the truth of what happened. I certainly never owned up to it.

All this fun couldn't last forever. As soon as I graduated and found a job, I got lazy and left roll-ups behind, switching back to boring old factory-made cigarettes. But to this day I always keep some rolling papers handy, just in case.

Steve Russell was raised by chain-smoking wolves in London, England. He quit the habit over a single weekend through sheer will power and the strategic application of blunt force. He now lives in semi-seclusion on the banks of the Olentangy, occasionally breaking cover to howl at the moon.

The Brown Mazda
David Middleton

The broken down Mazda RX-7 had sat on our lot for months. It could have been there for years for all I knew. I had no idea where it had come from. My parents owned a service station and restaurant on the Trans-Canada Highway about twenty kilometers or so from the Saskatchewan border. It was the early eighties and the recession still had us all in its grip. I assumed the Mazda had belonged to some poor soul who was heading west to Alberta to try and make a few bucks in the oilfields. There seemed to be a lot of that kind of talk back then. People would come into the gas station and trade things like Polaroid cameras for fuel. Just a little more fuel to push them further down that highway toward their dreams.

It had broken down on our lonely stretch of road. The owner had somehow got it as far as my dad's garage and upon hearing the cost of repair had either decided to abandon it or left with a promise of retrieving it when he had a few dollars in his pocket again. Either way the car was now a permanent fixture of the parking lot. It sat there on the gravel, backed up to the grass and left to the elements. Over time the tires deflated and the paint lost its lustre. The windshield was veiled in a coat of dust. Weeds began to grow out of the gravel around the tires, their roots sheltered by decaying rubber.

I had found out that it wasn't locked. To me it became a toy. I would sit in it and pretend to be hurtling through space or flying a World War 1 biplane. I imagined fixing it up when I was older and speeding around town. Sometimes I wondered what the person who owned it was like. What had become of them? Would they ever come back and take my toy away?

One thing I did know. They were smokers. The faint odor of cigarette smoke still clung to the fabric of the seats and the roof. I pulled open the dashboard ashtray just in front of the gear shift and there they were. Cigarette butts piled up to the rim. The brown filters beckoning and their squashed ends stubbed out and flattened like mushrooms. The acrid smell drifted from the ashes. Some were only half smoked. Others held a few flakes of tobacco in the final millimeters before the filter began. In the dark winter evenings after supper I would go out to the Mazda and dig around in the ashtray. I would find a butt worth smoking and light it up with a pack of matches I found in the glove box. I sat there in the seat sucking on the stale dried out cigarette, trying to get a few good drags out of it as I held it to my lips. My fingers pinched the very end of the filter as I tried to get every little flake of tobacco lit. Once it was gone I would dig through the ashtray again and find another good one. Other times I would just leave and save them for another night. Eventually, after I had re-smoked every butt at least once, the ashtray was filled with nothing but cottony brown dog ends. All the tobacco was gone. By then, however, I was ready to move on to the full size cigarettes I stole from my parent's packs one at a time so they would not notice. Behind the restaurant counter there were cigarette brands of all types on display. It was too easy to just scoot by and grab a pack and then head off outside. I would maybe join a friend or two and share. Other times I would just slip off into the trees and be alone.

The little brown Mazda eventually disappeared. Much like its mysterious arrival I don't know how it left us. I assumed that my dad had sold it or perhaps the owner suddenly re-appeared, having made his fortune in the oilfields of Alberta. Either way, my habit had long passed the stage of hiding out in a car and smoking cigarette butts left by a stranger.

David Middleton had big dreams growing up in a small Manitoba town. A former soldier, he currently works in the electronics field. He has a passion for technology and being in the outdoors. You can also find him struggling to make his guitar produce the music he hears in his head. He writes and blogs from his home in Northern Alberta.

Maybe I Should Have Stuck With the Leather Chaps
Jenn Dlugos

When I started high school, my "good girl" status was at a pathological level. I refused to dye my hair, pierce a body part, or even take a night off from homework in case the nuns at my Catholic school saw me through their invisible spyglass I was certain they hid in my religion textbook. While my friends had unleashed the Kraken of teen rebellion on their parents, I was Maryann of *The Babysitter's Club*. Hell, the fact that I know enough about *The Babysitter's Club* to make that reference should be adequate proof that I wasn't a Hell's Angel.

In retrospect, it was inevitable for me to be the late bloomer. I started kindergarten a year early, so I was always one year younger than my classmates. While all of the freshman girls dressed in cute teen outfits, I adopted the 90's grunge look of oversized flannel shirts and jeans to conceal any evidence I had a uterus at all. That, I decided, was all going to change at the school dance.

I had my school dance outfit planned for weeks. For my birthday I received a super rad black leather jacket and matching boots, which I planned to wear with skinny jeans, big hair, even bigger bangs, a black form-fitted shirt, and a thick, gold chain necklace. Unfortunately, my only thick gold chain also dangled a monstrous pendent of the Mickey Mouse symbol, but as long as no one looked too closely at the severed head of Mickey hanging from my neck, I looked like a bona fide badass. Almost. Something was missing. All of the parts of badassity were there, but the parts just didn't add up to the whole. Leather chaps were my first thought, but they didn't fit into my non-existent budget. No, I needed an accessory...a finisher...just that little extra boost to lift me over the fence of lameness and onto the sprawling lawn of coolness.

I needed a cigarette.

Only during the throes of teen angst does "chain smoking as a fashion accessory" make perfect sense. I'm not even sure why it popped into my head, as it wasn't exactly an area of expertise. Aside from my father shunning my Grandpa and his cigarette to the patio in subzero temperatures on Christmas morning, my only knowledge of smoking was that it was a favorite hobby of The Penguin from the Batman cartoons. I don't remember who bought me my cigarettes. I probably could have bought them myself, as my Amazonish height had been getting me into R-rated movies for two years already. The next morning, however, I had a brand new pack of cigarettes stuffed in my mini-backpack purse, ready for my perfectly executed swan dive into teen rebellion.

Much like with all perfectly planned swan dives in my life, I landed with a resounding belly flop.

My house had near-constant adult supervision. If my parents weren't home, one of my four grandparents were coming in and out for one reason or another. While this showed remarkable parenting skills on the part of Mom and Dad, it caused a significant scheduling snafu for my first cigarette. The school yard wasn't an option either, because if there was anything I feared more than my family finding me smoking, it was the nuns finding me smoking. The window of opportunity came at the butt crack of dawn one Saturday, when the entire family—grandparents included—headed out to my brother's swim meet. As soon as the front door locked behind them, I leaped out of bed and grabbed my mini-backpack. I knew I had hours before they came home, but I didn't want to waste a moment. For one, I needed to have enough time to get the smell off of me. Plus, I had no clue how long it actually took to smoke a cigarette. I could have asked one of my smoker friends, however teens aren't the best gauge of time, as evidenced by the common school bus debate of "how long does sex really last." The typical answer ranged anywhere between thirty seconds to eight hours, depending on the latest top secret intelligence released by the gossip hounds and braggarts from the last unsupervised party.

It was a balmy 9 degrees outside, so I opted to have my first cigarette in the garage. I took my seat on my pink Huffy, a bike that had no business still being in our garage, as I had long outgrown it, and my brother refused to ride it after making the discovery of "hot pink = for girls." I took one cigarette out of my fresh package and popped it in my mouth. We didn't have lighters in the house, so my only means to make fire was my parents' museum of matchbooks, all from local businesses that closed over 10 years ago. Honestly, I would have been better off rubbing two of my number 2 pencils together. I went through nearly an entire book of matches from Vinnie's Pizzeria—a restaurant I don't even remember existing—before one took pity on me and sparked a flame.

I expected my first cigarette to be an exquisite, sensory experience. I'd hear the gentle crackle of the fire as I placed the cigarette to my lips. My nasal cavities would flood with that enticing "first puff of a cigarette" smell. The cloud of smoke rocked gently over my taste buds until the smoke puffed out of my mouth in a beautifully shaped "O" that the girls in the James Bond movies effortlessly achieved.

What actually happened was much closer to the last 30 minutes of *The Exorcist*.

I don't remember how long the coughing fit lasted, though I'm certain the extra-terrestrial in *Alien* burst through the man's chest wall in less time. As my head hung pathetically between my legs in a desperate attempt to keep my lungs inside my chest cavity, I caught a glimpse in my bike's rear view mirror. Looking back at me was a six-foot tall girl on a hot pink kids' bike wearing an oversized flannel nightgown, Tweety Bird pajama pants, and monstrous Marvin the Martian slippers that she was damn close to hurling on.

Do you feel like a badass? My left brain chided me.

I shot back all the expletives I could think of, which ended up Morse coded through hacks and wheezes.

Nice mouth, my left brain continued. Oh, and by the way? Your hand is on fire.

During my bout of literally coughing up a lung, the tip of the cigarette in my left hand touched the second knuckle on my right hand, burning my skin. I dropped the cigarette, stomping it dead with an impromptu Tarantella dance, and frantically blew on my sizzling knuckle before it erupted into flames like Ghost Rider's head. I told my family that I burned myself on the toaster. In teen logic, it is better that your parents think you are an imbecile with small appliances than smoking a quarter of a cigarette in the garage.

I went to the dance that night in my planned badass outfit. I tossed the cigarettes into a communal ashtray sometime that afternoon. As it turned out, I didn't need them. When I entered the dance, I was flooded by ooohs, aaahs, and pleased looks of surprise at this New Jenn. For the first time, I was the center of attention. I felt confident. I talked to kids I had never talked to in school. I danced, instead of being a wallflower. I even had my first high school dance with a cute boy, who was granted a second dance when he told me he liked my perfume. As soon as I got home, I ripped off the binding clothes and slipped back into my comfortable flannel and oversized jeans. New Jenn was fun and exciting, but for the safety of my lungs and remaining unscathed knuckles, she was probably best let out in small, controlled doses. Plus her costume choices were too damn binding.

The teen years are fraught with inner turmoil and punctuated with light bulb moments of self-discovery. My first cigarette taught me an important mantra—don't try to be someone I'm not. There are many healthier ways I could have achieved this realization—yoga, an improv class, trying on a form-fitting flannel, perhaps. At least my first cigarette was a dumb decision that offers a continuous education. Every time I look down at my right hand and see the very faint scar above my second knuckle, I'm reminded of another very important mantra: "If you play with fire, you're going to get burned."

When the pack of cigarettes she bought on her 18th birthday went stale in her purse, Jenn Dlugos knew she was not going to be a smoker and returned to her previous vices of lottery scratch tickets and Reese's products. She is an award-winning screenwriter and is a semi-finalist in the Lifetime

Television Unscripted Development Pipeline. Jenn is the co-editor of the award-winning "Woe" humor book series, including Mug of Woe: Tales to Realize Your Life is Awesome and Woe of the Road: Tales To Make You Never Want to Leave Your House. All of the Woe books are available on Amazon and Kindle. You can stalk her on her website thescriptscribe.com or on Twitter @jenndlugos.

Memoir in Menthol
Erica Deis

I had vowed never to smoke. My mom had been
a career smoker, the kind of person who collected
ashtrays from every place she visited. I'd get thrown
into the car for afternoon drives to look at "autumn
leaves". Fearful of any ventilation that could
potentially muss her hair, she rolled the windows
tight. Cigarettes, Aqua Net and White Linen have
the same fume-like properties of ammonia and
bleach. I spent my childhood half buzzed from the
combination.

At least once a day I was sent to the market
across two lanes of traffic with a note. In the 80's,
cigarettes could be purchased by eight year olds as
long as they had a note. If I was lucky, I'd get thrown
a buck extra so at least I could buy a candy bar for
my trouble. That intermittent reward kept me going.

At thirteen I was exiled from the trappings of
Catholic School. I became a public school kid. In
Cranston, Rhode Island, this translated into fitting

in by donning two different pairs of day-glo socks at a time in an alternate pattern on each foot over skin tight jeans and high-tops. I bought shirts that I tried to convince my mother adequately covered my midriff.

If you walked into any school bathroom without paying attention, you could get sprayed in the face full blast with force of hairspray that eventually doomed the environment. It had the same ingredients people used to side their houses. I would inspect hairspray bottles for vinyl laminate.

I was allowed to get a perm. I had long hair, so this would involve "kitty cornering" rollers during the process. I became known as a girl with some of the biggest hair in junior high, and this was a laudable award, trumping any academic achievement or sports trophy. Waking two hours before class, I used a pick and a blow dryer, spraying on coat after coat of LA Looks. I had to wash my hair twice, once in the evening and once in the morning, lest be left with a mop of chipped flakes.

I was befriended by a girl whose father was a mayor in another town. She went to swanky places like Europe and Newport. Her parents hated me. I chewed gum constantly and wore jeans with the zipper up the back. Her father took me to Provincetown at his daughter's nagging, his eyes sizing me up, audibly sighing.

Heather looked the part of a virginal angel. She knew college boys that had no idea we were fourteen. Maybe they knew, but they pretended not to. We drove around the Cape with a breathy George Michael tape blaring. We tested the speed limit in their Camaros to Race Point. Heather announced she was going to go skinny dipping. I hadn't gotten over my self-consciousness, so I watched her on the beach, pacing back and forth with a sex hungry letch with acne. His face reminded me of Freddy Krueger.

Heather's mom worked a lot, so we had the run of the house. One afternoon, Heather invited over about ten of her friends from private school...and me. One of them pulled out a pack of Virginia Slims, certainly pilfered from her mother.

Someone in the group offered me one. I declined.

Every morning my mother insisted on braids. She would yank my hair into braids so tight they gave me a headache. I had memories of being seven and having smoke loom in giant clouds around me in our narrow bathroom without windows. I was the only kid in the second grade who went to school reeking of butts.

"You don't smoke?" Heather taunted. "You look like you smoke."

I took this as a compliment. I probably shouldn't have.

Everyone was staring at me. If I refused, I would be mocked. One girl giggled. Already feeling like an outsider in this moneyed crowd, I needed to secure my place as token Rebel. I took the thin cigarette.

Striking out lighting me with the two remaining matches (someone forgot to steal a lighter), Heather began scheming.

"But I need to teach you how to smoke," she informed.

"Use the stove," one girl recommended.

She turned the burner on. I could get through this, I chided myself. I probably had scarred lung tissue from secondhand smoke. I tensed as the burner grew orange.

I leaned down to light my cigarette.

I would be cool.

My hair ignited. The spark spread through my hair like a brush fire.

The kids started screaming and whacking at my bouffant. My head was aflame. The smell of singed, lacquered hair filled the kitchen.

It was worse than any car ride.

When the fire was properly snuffed out, the group burst into hysterics.

I had to redeem myself. Armed with idiocy that can only be found in adolescents, I handed my cigarette to Heather. She was slightly less flammable.

None of them needed to teach me how to smoke. I sucked in the cigarette. After coughing and nearly throwing up, I was part of the Smoking Club.

A few months later, Heather's mother called to inform my mother that she had found matches and Merit Menthol Ultra Lights under Heather's bed. Since those were the brand that my mother smoked, she was certain that I had somehow convinced her poor, innocent daughter to acquire a nasty habit.

"I've smelled smoke on her, you know," Heather's mom fumed.

"I'll talk to her," my mom vowed. For some reason, she never did.

I had to sneak out of Heather's before her mother came home. After a neighbor reported a big-haired girl in colorful socks leaving the premises, I was banished altogether.

"You have to understand," Heather sniffed. "I have to maintain a certain reputation. My father is a mayor, after all."

The next time she went to Provincetown, I was not invited.

I was moving to Western Massachusetts anyway. I made an entrance into that school. The kids wore khakis with more consistency than the rich kids in

Rhode Island. Instead of viewing me as a big-haired freak, I became the mysterious girl from the Big City. Boys hounded me, convinced the height of my hair meant accessible promiscuity. Girls wanted to be my friend. I exaggerated stories of pot smoking and beer drinking. I think I even threw in a fable about hanging out in bars.

Since my mother was now purchasing me cartons of Newport Stripes, aptly named for the pretty pastel stripes on the filter, I illicitly sold cigarettes to my new friends. Crouched in the window on sleep overs, I would pull them out.

"We all smoke in Rhode Island," I would tell them. Wanting to absorb the glamour I had invented, they would look at me warily. And then smoke.

I'm pretty sure Heather doesn't smoke anymore. Now that it's become tantamount to booting heroin in polite society, I'm sure she still maintains her image. It was as ingrained in her as churning butter is in Amish culture.

I see smokers, ashamed, still crouched behind their cars, out of eyeshot of their children. We now are given "designated smoking areas" where we can be corralled, being sociopathic deviants.

I began smoking again when my soon-to-be husband smoked. At first, I complained of his sour smell, but after a glass of wine or two I would join. We would go outside together and at first, share a cigarette. Then we would fight over who smoked more and was squandering the family fortune.

"You take a lot of trash out, Mommy," my son said one day with a furrowed brow.

"I try to keep up on things," I told him. He shook his head and returned to his DS.

I will quit. It's too expensive, and there will come a day soon my son will not be pacified with a story about mounds of invisible garbage.

But there are times I want to feel like a subversive rogue. My life filled with Easter egg hunts and Disney movies, I still rebel. I smoke.

Erica Deis is a native of Northampton, Massachusetts. She has lived in Boston, New York and Cape Cod, but has been lured back to Rhode Island by the crack-like properties of Fellini's Pizza and Del's Lemonade. Erica a.k.a "Charm School Debutante" has been a vocational counselor for people with Prader-Willi syndrome, an abominable waitress, a histrionically happy customer service representative for health insurance, a people whisperer, and an animal advocate. As well as being a University of Rhode Island alumnus, Erica is a Special Programs Coordinator with the Rhode Island Film Festival. She is currently working on her first screenplay. She has written short stories, long-winded complaints, and several editorials that ended up on the bottom of some very prominent litter boxes.

Straggler
Kris Earle

I graduated from UMass-Amherst in 1993 "cum laude." That is UMass code for "Although you abused your body with booze and smokes these past four years, luckily your liver, lungs and other bodily functions are still intact, so congratulations." Sure, my lungs weren't virgin pink and my liver wasn't as juicy as it was in 1989, but I made it. I've even got a diploma that arrived in the mail five months after graduation to prove it.

I was back visiting Amherst in May '94 to visit my friend Steve, who was graduating that weekend. Steve was another fine study to make the case for substance abuse, however Steve was only at UMass-Amherst the last two years of his college run, so his body was still mildly in love with him. Mine was starting to call me a vicious bitch and screaming out for help. At UMass-Amherst, Drinking 101 is a required course the first semester that both Steve and myself passed with flying colors as all the best

UMass-Amherst graduates normally do. By this point I was in the graduate courses, working a day job the past year and keeping up with my aggressive social schedule at night, including these binge weekends at UMass. Smoking 101 was never a required course; however, having a pack of smokes that you could distribute to friends during a night out made you the equivalent of a Jedi Knight. At the time they were $2 a pack, but it was rare to see many students with them. Although carrying a lighter seemed to also be a requirement for every student, having actual cigarettes was rare. When you did have them though and you whipped 'em out at just the right moment, everyone loved you and we would all smoke and drink and chat and smoke and drink and chat, maybe make out with a stranger, take a nap, eat an entire pizza, prank call the asshole neighbor, what-have-you. It was bliss.

I met Steve at the old house he was renting out. It was a relatively large run down old farmhouse on the way to Hadley, kind of outside the beaten path of UMass. We decided to stick in for the start of the night, drink ten or twelve beers, then definitely head out later and get all fucked up.

Steve shared the place with at least two other guys. I say at least, because back in college days, no one was really sure how many roommates they really had. There were the ones who were "official" because they or their parents were responsible enough to pay the rent, and there were the gypsies who would wander in and out like it was a summer of love 60's commune. Sometimes you'd have 8-10 roommates who you only knew on a first name basis. There would be so much hair in the bathtub drain that it would take days to drain after a quick shower. Though being a house full of 21 year old guys, the tub wasn't utilized as much as it should have been. Personal hygiene was not a required course at UMass-Amherst.

The night started off with a few beers. Bud Lights. A little primer. Shoot the shit, play some pool, drink some beers. Repeat.

What was cool was it was just me and Steve. Since they weren't graduating until next year, all his roommates had already gone home for the summer.

What wasn't cool is that there was shit everywhere. Dishes in the sink. Dishes in the tub. Rotten fruit. Blackflies. Empty beers. Random cat. Carelessly discarded underwear which was recently flung and abandoned into the corner of the dining room. Half full beers (stragglers). Some indescribable stains on the wall that were either the result of sex or a sacrifice, possible both, most likely human. More stragglers.

We didn't care. We were young and were used to everything around us smelling like a rendering plant. We cracked a few bottles and played some pool. Everything was going swimmingly. Then it happened.

I placed my beer down on the pool table next to a straggler. Mistake.

Now a straggler isn't always a bad thing. For those unfamiliar, a straggler is a leftover beer that isn't quite empty, though it's hardly ever full. It can be found in either glass bottle or plastic cup form at almost all college keggers in its fresh born-on-date form. But it's also common that it has been left over from the night before. I experienced the early stages of alcoholism firsthand when I saw freshmen come by and sneak a few stragglers into their hands and chug 'em down, not caring what kind of beer it was, what nasty lips were on the cup or bottle and not noticing whether anything was discarded into the bottle.

I was always afraid of the stragglers, but I did take note and used them when necessary throughout my college career. I would be doing a disservice to college students at party Universities around the globe if I did not confess to you, dear reader, that I myself spent a few nights those freshmen-senior years where a keg ran dry and the stragglers kept my buzz on for the night. I have no shame.

So I placed my Bud Light right next to another Bud Light. A straggler.

A straggler that I later learned happened to be one from a party held the previous weekend before, so it wasn't quite as fresh as it could have been. A straggler that probably had a few bonus sea monkeys floating in it since it had been fermenting in its own juices all during this eighty degree week in mid-May.

I lined up my cue ball, sank the eight. Success! Great game, Steve.

Reached for my beer in celebration, not looking. Asshole.

Grabbed the straggler by mistake. Chugged it.

Inside this five ounce filled, warm as piss, sea monkey laden Bud Light straggler was also a gigantic cigarette butt. The goddamn thing had to be at least twelve inches long and damn near two inches thick. It came out of the bottle with such ease as if it almost belonged in my throat and sailed into its harbor with only sea monkey bacteria as its lubrication.

I looked at Steve in horror.

I somehow was able to skirt around the ciggie butt in the mouth all through my four years at UMass. I always looked before I drank a straggler, gave the bottle a little shake, the plastic a once over. At worst, some leftover floaty was found and the straggler remained where I found it, left behind as undrinkable. I must've been rusty though during my time away from UMass, because I let this one happen. I drank it. Ew.

I opened my mouth as wide as I could and half dropped and half puked it all out, the cigarette falling onto the unwashed carpet like a log racing down Niagara Falls.

After a hack, I looked up at Steve and said:

"I've always been scared that I'd swallow a leftover ciggie in a straggler!"

Then a pause. A thought.

"You know what, though? It wasn't that bad. Let's play pool!"

Steve laughed his ass off and got me a fresh Bud Light, sans cigarette butt. We left a few stragglers for his roommates for the next party and hit the town. The remainder of the night was uneventful but the next morning I did leave some soiled underwear in the corner for good measure. Just another great weekend binge drinking at UMass-Amherst. Best college ever.

Kris Earle is America's Best Kept Secret. When he's not drinking, he's trying to quit cigarettes. Kris once performed standup in front of the current President of the United States, Barack Obama. At another more recent show, he performed in front of his mother, Donna Wolfenden. Kris likes to keep it real. You can find Kris doing sketch comedy, standup, and improv all around the globe. It would behoove you to know that Kris blends in like Waldo though, so look for him with a keen eye. Kris also hosts a weekly radio show called "Time Travel" from 5-7 p.m. every Wednesday on 91.5FM, WMFO in Medford, Ma.. You can download past shows or listen live at wmfo.org. Or don't. But that's your decision and a poor one.

I Smoke to Prove I'm Alive
Linda Siniard

My dad stopped smoking cigarettes and driving
his Indian motorcycle the day he found out my mom
was pregnant with my older brother. The year was
1950. One of my favorite photos of the two of them
shows them leaning against the beast out front of
my mom's childhood home in Birmingham,
Alabama. Young, happy, in love, and a motorcycle –
what could be better? More hopeful? The
motorcycle was just a backdrop for a life of wild
abandon for both of them – him, from a highly
structured, professional, and privileged family
framework, and her, from "the other side of the
tracks" - one of chaos and uncertainty.

Daddy was a practical man, and with a doctor
and nurse as parents, he may well have known that
smoking was a choice that could end up with
hospitals and a slow, painful death. Given the times,
though, he may not have even have given it a
passing thought. No one talked about cigarettes,

heart disease, respiratory illnesses, and cancer being connected with smoking much back then.

According to my mom as to why he quit, he thought it was a nasty habit that smelled bad, and didn't want to subject his soon-to-be-born kid to it. Mom, on the other hand, only stopped smoking briefly during her pregnancy. From what I'm told, she barely got home from the hospital before she lit up again.

My brother, Emmitt, was born in April of 1951, and has never smoked a cigarette. He did take me for a late-night ride on a friend's motorcycle when we were teenagers, driving fast down Sierra Madre Boulevard in Pasadena, California. I think it was the last time he took such a risky chance of his body ending up splayed out on the asphalt - bones, muscle, and fluids distributed to the far reaches of the roadway and the surrounding fields due to a potential confrontation with a moving vehicle larger than ours, or any error in physical coordination. My mom and me, and our willingness to throw caution to the wind, well, that's another story. "Pass me the lighter, Lindy."

I've been smoking since I was fourteen years old. I had always sworn I wouldn't pick up the habit. I hated the smell, the smoke circling around my face, the look of the paper stick hanging out of someone's mouth. I just didn't get it. Until...I did.

When I was a kid, my mom used to wake me up for school by flipping on the light in my bedroom accompanied by the smoke of a cigarette, greeting me much as an implement of torture greets the prisoner. I would recoil under the light of the bare 75-watt bulb and the noxious odor, hiding my head under the covers. If I didn't bolt out of bed within minutes, I could count of her returning, which meant more of the unpleasantness. At the time, I don't even think I was aware of how much I wanted to wake up to the smell of a new dawn, to bacon and eggs on the stove, to a hopeful send-off from Mama for a good day at school, bereft of the smell of burning tobacco.

I learned a lot when I moved out of her house at seventeen. And, then, I relearned that my past would follow me into my future, but, with different tools for coping, different hopes for my future. She didn't have many. She accepted long ago that life was hard, and she lived to prove it.

At first, I only tried to mimic the look and feel of smoking. It was the 1960s, and smoking was still a sign of the new feminist movement, glamour, and independence. We could smoke because no one told us we shouldn't or couldn't. Now, I hide my smoking like the addict I've become...lighting up in my car, or in my backyard, in restaurant parking lots more than 25 feet from the doorway, or in the company of other smokers in out-of-the-way places.

How many blouses and dresses have I burned holes in? Not that many, really. I'm a careful smoker, one that cleans off the dashboard to my car regularly, washes ashtrays daily, and assures all empty cigarette boxes go into the recycle bin immediately. But, when it happens, when an ash lands on my clothes on my drive to work or a gala fundraising event, I think of the big red A of "The Scarlet Letter" and wonder how much it's worth. Right now, smoking is worth being considered a pariah. I smoke. Fuck you and your judgments.

Most, but not all of the important people in my life, smoke. Some of them smoke daily, regularly, addictively. Some smoke only when they're drinking. Some of them smoke cigarettes, more of them smoke pot, and plenty of them smoke both. As I see it, ritual is the key to their intentions, though some of them don't make the connection.

Lea, one of my oldest friends, who is half Native American and half Irish (yes, a genuine red-headed Indian) is a militant smoker. Long ago, she told me the reason she smokes is to prove she's alive. When I asked her to explain that statement when we were in our late twenties, she said that she's never been sure she's actually living here on the Planet, but because she smokes, she can always see the smoke being released from her lungs. That, alone, proved she was alive. Huh. When I'm most uncertain if I'm alive, which since my 20-year-old son died a few years back, happens more frequently, I remember what Lea said those many years ago. And, I light a cigarette. And, pretend Owen is there lighting up with me. Because, he, too, smoked to prove he was alive.

Smokers tell me I'm not a "real" smoker because I'll smoke a bunch, then stop for days, sometimes weeks. I don't have an intention to "quit" I just don't feel like smoking. I don't miss it when I'm breathing air rather than nicotine and the many other carcinogens. I even hate being around it, can't stand the smell, the mess. The sun will come up and I'll wish I had a pack of American Spirit orange cigarettes in the house. I'll drink my coffee on the deck, write my papers, catch up with email, listen to music, shower, dress, and drive to the smoke shop, hoping the pack I buy isn't stale. At over $7.00 a pack in California, smoking my brand of cigarettes is a commitment and a financial deficit. The health deficit doesn't often figure into the cost, though I'm cognizant of the deterioration of mind, body, and spirit in the act. That is, until my chest hurts and I hear my lungs wheeze.

When I listen to "Hotel California" by the Eagles, I light a cigarette, even if I don't feel like smoking. Why? Because I hear "those voices calling from far away". The voices of my past come with morning coughs (mine now), light switches flipping on in the new-dawn light, swirling smoke near my bedroom door looking for the "passage back to the place I was before". Besides the stories of my mom and our smoking mornings on the patio in San Diego before she died, I have similar stories about most of the rest of my family. How did we become a family of smokers? Not sure, I just know that we have this thing in common. Except, for Emmitt, my brother. He never picked up the habit. How did he escape this thing, this habit, this addiction, this familiarity with our dead ancestors? I don't know, but I often wish I had the same aversion to smoking.

And, for all the dead ones, part of the reason I still smoke is so I can feel close to them – Owen especially, my son that died two weeks before his

21st birthday. It's a given, that in the bereavement community, we, the survivors, often pick up habits from the departed, just to remember, to feel connected to them. Owen would probably say that's bullshit, but I can tell you that smoking on my deck late at night, searching the sky for signs of tomorrow's calling, is a connection to our many nights together doing the same. Owen and I, smoking in the late-night hours, on the deck or in the backyard, looking up at the stars, and wondering what's out there – those were the days, those are the memories. And, I'm okay with that.

I rarely try to quit smoking. More, I try to live in collaboration with smoking. Once in a while, I light up a cigarette in a public place where I know my actions will be seen as offensive, or even in some geographies, illegal. I get a kick out it, like my teenage-self smoking in the alley across the street from school next to the church. It's a defiant act, a moment of rebellion, a statement of independence, time, and space.

I'm standing on the street, I light a cigarette, and I smoke to prove I'm alive. I watch the smoke emanating from my body and in that visible, noxious gas, I know I'm still here on the Planet.

Anyone who tries to stop me...well, don't. I might just blow smoke in your face.

Linda applies inconsistency to her life as her spiritual practice. She is a fervent believer that beliefs can be limiting to the magic, music, and mystery of life. She believes she will quit smoking someday. Just like all beliefs, there is no evidence to prove this.

The Benefits of Smoking:
The Corporate Years (circa 2002)
Lizzy Miles

Four months ago my boyfriend Kevan decided
that we were going to quit smoking together. After
four months of daily discussions of how much we
were craving a smoke, I've come to the conclusion
that one of us will succeed and one won't. Today I
cheated and had a cigarette. Kevan has been fine
since he got the nicotine out of his system. I'm not.
For me, it was never the nicotine to begin with – it
was the benefits. Yes, benefits. There are benefits
to smoking that only a smoker or ex-smoker could
understand and that's what I miss the most.

The first benefit is the networking. This is best
understood in an office environment. The smokers
have a club that crosses all departments and all
levels. I work for a large Midwestern financial
services organization. There are five hundred
people in my building and there are many people in
other departments like accounting and legal that I
know that I would not know otherwise, except that

we've shared a dry spot under a tent at 3:15 on a rainy Monday afternoon talking about movies and inhaling nicotine for fifteen minutes. This is how I met the office transsexual, "Melissa," a 200 pound broad shouldered permed blond who frequently wore black leather skirts and low cut sleeveless blouses to work. The very first time I heard Melissa talk about her life I was hooked. We were in the smoking tent in the patio outside the cafeteria.

"My ex girlfriend and I had a psychic connection. She could tell when I wanted something to drink and she would just go get it for me. After we broke up, I got mad at her and put a hex on her so that she would never find anyone who loves her again." She was talking to another woman whom I didn't know who wasn't really paying attention to her.

"Hex?" I interrupted. I couldn't help myself.

"Yeah, I'm a witch and I have psychic abilities." Holy shit, she was serious. I didn't quite know what to make of her, but I was intrigued so I would seek her out any time I was outside. Melissa was one of the few other people who didn't think I was a freak for my interest in the supernatural.

"So Melissa, why can't I see ghosts?" I was into this ghost phase and I had been reading a ton of books about spirits, but I have never personally had an experience. I didn't really expect her to have an answer.

"Look into my eyes," she commanded. I stared into her pale blue warm eyes for a long pause. "It will happen. It's not your time yet. When the time is right, you'll see. You're not ready yet." Somehow, I believed her.

Melissa eventually moved to another building, and I lost touch with her. If she came back to our building, I would probably take up smoking just to talk to her again.

***

There is no typical smoker, so by meeting other smokers, I was meeting a wide variety of people. The CFO of my company smokes and because of an innocuous conversation about a local mall two years ago during a smoke break, we are now on a 'hello in the hallway' acquaintance.

Even if you are on a smoke break with people you already know from your own department, there is something about the environment that leads to disclosure. If you smoke as well and you happen to be out on the patio at the same time, you are going to be privy to some pretty juicy information.

"Melissa almost got fired today, she leaned over Brad's desk and her boob fell out." I try not to look at Heather's gray teeth as she leans down to whisper. "Brad was so mad – he reported it to HR right away."

"How did you find this out?" I suspected Heather found out from Brad on a different smoke break – he was a fellow smoker. "Why would Brad care? He's gay." Everyone knew Brad was gay, mostly because he would openly check out other guys at work.

"Apparently gay men don't like transsexuals. Anyways – he can't stand her."

"Melissa doesn't even like guys, she likes girls." I knew this because Melissa had told me about her many girlfriends on one of our smoke breaks.

"Well anyways, she has a few days off without pay." Heather shrugged and walked towards the ashtray to put her cigarette out.

"I can't believe Brad would report it." I swiped my badge to get in the door.

"He thinks she did it on purpose." We both shrugged and parted until the next break.

***

Being a smoker at the right time is almost as good as the proverbial 'fly on the wall' – during that first rush of nicotine, most people spill their guts. Many people choose to smoke when they are pissed off about something. It doesn't work to just go out and stand and not smoke with someone who is smoking. There is something that bonds the two smokers. It's US against THEM.

***

Because smoking is so unpopular now, there is a band-together mentality with smokers. We are a dying breed. No pun intended. You can get a seat quickly in a restaurant now in the smoking section because no one wants to sit there anymore. I don't sit in smoking anymore because I can't stand the smell, but mostly because I'm fiercely jealous of the after-dinner light up.

A lot of ex-smokers complain about the weight gain they've had as a result of quitting. There are some statistics about nicotine and it being an appetite suppressant but I don't think that's the real reason that people gain weight. When I was a smoker I always ended my meal with a cigarette. Now that I don't smoke, I don't know when the meal has ended and I keep eating. You can ask just about any smoker: If you have 10 minutes in the car before you have to be somewhere, would you rather smoke or eat? I know that I would choose smoking over food most of the time. Parties are the worst because there is so much food to nibble on. When I smoke, I don't have the desire to nibble because I've been occupied with smoking.

While we are talking about our bodies, I would like to say that I also think I had better breath when I was a smoker. All smokers, when they hear this, smile and nod. Literally, was my breath better? Maybe not. But when I smoked, I was so much more conscious of having bad breath from smoking that I took greater steps to make sure my breath was clean. I always had gum or mints. Secondary to that, of course, was that smoking ruins your sense of smell, so if I did have bad breath, I couldn't smell my own breath anyway.

***

When you smoke, you will always be prepared with a lighter for candles and concerts. Also, smoking also offers a conversation starter in public places for smokers and non smokers alike.

"Do I smell cloves? It reminds me of church."

"Who is smoking cloves? Oh it's you. I used to smoke those in high school."

"Does anyone have a light?"

"Those smell so good. I can't stand regular cigarettes, but those are ok."

"What is that smell? It smells like pot." and also...

"What is that God-awful smell?"

***

Perhaps the saddest benefit to smoking is that it really did give me something to look forward to. At my last job my friend and I had times where we would go for a smoke break every day. Ten-thirty, after lunch and three o'clock. Sometimes there would be ten or fifteen of us who would all go outside at the same time.

_____EMAIL_____

TO: All Smokers

From: Elizabeth Miles

Subject: Time

Message: 3:15 on the patio. It's a beautiful day. Be there!

_____

There really isn't the enjoyment factor with anything else since I have quit smoking. It was a tiny perk, but a perk all the same. It was something to look forward to. "Let's go get a cup of coffee!!!"

doesn't quite have the same punch. Shit, I don't even like coffee.

So here I am, teetering on the edge of four months smoke free. I'm fifteen pounds fatter and I don't feel any healthier at all. It seems like you should feel a difference if it's going to be rewarding.

Today, though, the lone cigarette has had a lasting effect. I can't get the cigarette smell out of my hands. I can smell it now because I've regained my sense of smell. I swear my eyes are irritated. My stomach is queasy and I have heartburn. My throat is scratchy and I have this dry cough that I haven't had in ... well... four months. My body has rebelled this relapse. I feel horrible. So why do I want another?

This is the original story that inspired the book. All names were changed to protect the smokers. More than a decade later, Lizzy is in the same situation with just having quit smoking.

The Benefits of Smoking Part II:
In Search of Celebrities
Lizzy Miles

When I first wrote the Benefits of Smoking in
2002, it had not even occurred to me that one of the
benefits of smoking would be to rub elbows with a
"celebrity."

In 2004, my friend Lori and I went to Los
Angeles for vacation. At the time, we were both
tabloid readers and had high hopes that if we placed
ourselves in all the right locations, we would
eventually see someone who had been on the cover
of *Us Weekly* magazine.

We stayed at the Hyatt West Hollywood, which
is now the Andaz West Hollywood. According to the
websites that tell you where to see stars, this was the
place of legend in the 1970s where all the famous
musicians had stayed. We laughed when we were
told that the balcony doors could not be opened
more than a few inches because people in the past
had thrown things on the street. Keith Richards
supposedly threw a television out the window. Jim

Morrison and Little Richards lived there. We imagined that we were staying in a room that a rock star had trashed. Perhaps that was true, as the room had seen better days.

We got haircuts at a high-end celebrity salon. The stylist, as most people in L.A., was blasé about all the celebs that had been in his salon. Perhaps in his mind, he was the celebrity; actresses were paying him to make them look good. Three hundred and fifty dollars later, I had a new cut and color, but the experience was underwhelming.

Lori and I walked along Melrose Avenue and even ate lunch at Fred Segal. It was a bit like the excitement of playing a slot machine for me, I was waiting for the big payoff. At the time, the jackpot would have been a Paris Hilton sighting, as she was the "it" girl of the day. Seems funny now. Later, we also walked by the well-known see-and-be seen restaurant, The Ivy, just in case Ben Affleck and Jennifer Lopez were having a reunion lunch that day.

The Saddle Ranch was down the street from our hotel and was a filming location for countless television shows and movies. If you have ever seen a show after 1999 with someone riding a mechanical bull, chances are it was filmed there. We thought we would see someone there because it was supposedly a popular hangout. Except that we went in the middle of the afternoon and it was pretty dead. Our waitress enthralled us with tales about a reality show wrap party she would be attending that evening. Then she convinced us to get the "house special" drinks. Sure enough when we got our bill, we were charged for top shelf liquor. Toto, we're not in Kansas anymore. We must have been easy marks.

I forget why I was out and about by myself, but I when I walked by the Starbucks on Sunset, I was convinced that I saw a celebrity sitting down there reading a paper. It was before the days of smart phones, so we did not have internet for me to look up who it was. It was driving me absolutely nuts trying to think of who it was, but I knew he looked familiar. Not a leading man, but someone who was always an ensemble bad guy character. Later when Lori went back with me, the same man was behind the counter. It turned out he was just a Starbuck's employee that happened to look like someone else.

Of all the places we went to see celebrities, we never expected our celebrity sighting to be at the House of Blues. We were at the House of Blues on Sunset Boulevard waiting for the Blondie show to start. Lori had gone off to use the restroom and when she came back she told me that she found an out of the way restroom that had no line. She took me upstairs and sure enough, unlike the downstairs restroom, this one was empty. When we walked out of the restroom, we saw a door to a smoking area right outside, a balcony. When we first went out there, it was not crowded, but it seemed to fill up fast. The California people were all too-cool-for-school. Leather pants, leopard print, sunglasses at night. They were the early hipsters, before it became cliché.

Gradually I came to the realization that everyone else on the balcony was wearing wristbands. There was a security guard at the door that hadn't been there before. We realized that we had happened upon an exclusive group. VIP perhaps? We knew that if we left we would not be able to return to this people-watching paradise.

There was an "older" man in his mid-40s sitting next to us and he started a conversation. Normally, this would creep me out but he really did not seem like he was flirting with either of us. He was conservatively dressed in a button down-shirt and slacks, as if he had come from work. He talked about his family and mentioned his wife owned a big hot-dog chain. We told him we were from Ohio and we had never been to L.A. before. We confided that we had ended up on the balcony by accident and that we did not belong.

"I'll get you wristbands," he said. "Follow me."

So we followed him. Lori, when she was wandering around earlier, had previously tried to enter the Foundation Room. She had been sternly told that it was VIP only. She did not want to face the security guards again.

"That's okay, really. We'll just go watch the show." She does not like to impose on anyone and to her, this was an imposition. To me, an adventure. We followed the man to the security guard where he told the guard we needed wristbands. The guard said no.

The man said something very close to, "Don't you know who I am?" and then proceeded to tell the guard who he was. The guard persisted in his resistance and the man asked for a supervisor. The whole time, Lori was saying, "really, it's no big deal. We don't need them."

But the man would not relent. His pride had been challenged. He persisted and we got our wristbands. By this time the concert had started. The man then took us into the Foundation Room. Even though the Blondie concert was downstairs, there was a jazz band playing in this room. It was dark. I think we had a drink.

Finally the man said, "Do you want to see the concert?"

We said yes.

So he led us into another room with big couches and a big screen television. People were milling about watching the concert on television, even though it was going on right in the same building. We were shocked! While we were sitting on the plush couches, we started to hear a buzz about the room.

"Andy Dick's here."

"Andy Dick is at the concert."

"Andy Dick is outside."

I think the man noticed that we were intrigued and he said, "Do you want to go outside?" We said yes and went back out to the VIP smoking area.

I ended up sitting next to Andy Dick's security guard. Andy Dick was on the other side of him. The man told us the security guard was less for Andy Dick and more to protect others from Andy Dick. That's what he said, anyways. Andy seemed harmless enough to me. We were close enough to hear everything that anyone said to Andy. Mostly it was a lot of sucking up.

"Hi Andy, I loved your show News Radio."

"Hi Andy, do you remember me, we met at a party last summer."

"You're sooooo funny!"

This was the closest that Lori and I had ever been to a celebrity and we were lapping up the entertainment. We had forgotten about the concert. Andy Dick was the show and we watched him interact with people all night.

Towards the end of the evening, a woman's coat was abandoned. Lori, who had enjoyed a few cocktails, went up to Andy Dick and asked if it was his coat. He took it and started carrying it around. I think eventually he realized that it wasn't his and he threw it down with a flourish.

This one time Los Angeles "celebrity" encounter would not have ever happened were it not for my smoking habit. This is one benefit of smoking that I will not soon forget.

Intent to Smoke
Lizzy Miles

I just smoked my "last" cigarette. Okay it was a cigar. A clove cigar. Are you disgusted? I was. It is out of desperation that I smoked these. You see, I was smoke-free for so long. Relatively speaking. I only smoked when I went to Las Vegas once or twice a year, but then I would smoke a pack a day. When I came back from my trip, I would quit cold turkey every time. Seems reasonable enough, right? I justified the smoking by telling myself that I was already inhaling secondhand smoke in the casino anyways.

The rule of only smoking in Vegas worked well for several years. Then something happened: in 2009, President Obama made my treasured clove cigarettes illegal to sell in the United States. He said flavored cigarettes were "gateway" cigarettes that enticed young smokers. Yes, they were enticing, perhaps. I never did smoke regular cigarettes and still won't.

Fortunately, there was forewarning that the law was going into effect and that Fall I stocked up before my Vegas trip. All was well until I finished my last pack. What to do? I looked online and found that I could order them online directly from Indonesia. The process was a little scary. At first my credit card denied the order, assuming they were protecting me from fraud. They didn't know it, but they were protecting my lungs. A phone call with the credit card company cleared up the misunderstanding, and the charge appeared on the statement as if I had spent the night at a luxurious resort in Bali.

When my three cartons of Sampoerna clove cigarettes arrived, I was a bit overwhelmed. I had never purchased a carton before and it indicated a serious intent to smoke. However, I was also delighted because the cost per pack was significantly lower than in the United States, about $2 cheaper. I was still a non-smoker at the time, so the cartons went into the freezer for the next Vegas trip. Those cartons lasted me three years, despite the increasing frequency of my jaunts to Vegas.

Though in my heart I know I only have myself to blame for my habit, there are others I outwardly accuse of being "bad influences." Last year we moved into a new house and the new neighbors were very friendly and very heavy smokers. It was hard to be with them and to watch them enjoy every last puff of their smokes. I had always been a social smoker and I wanted to smoke with them.

It was a week before one Las Vegas trip where I broke the Vegas-only rule. I was sitting on my neighbor's patio and I thought to myself, "What the heck – I'll be smoking in Vegas next week anyway." I walked back over to my house, dug into the freezer and pulled out a pack. That night I think I chain-smoked three or four cloves in a row.

The rest of the remaining packs from the first Indonesia purchase were puffed away in Vegas and then afterwards. We had a party and my friend's boyfriend was visiting from out of town and he smoked a lot. In his presence I usually was strong, but when the neighbors came over, the cloves came out. Although mostly non-smokers, many of the people at the party were people we had been to Las Vegas with on multiple occasions. The party almost felt like Vegas. I dug into the freezer again.

On my last Vegas trip, I had less than two packs of clove cigarettes left so I had to supplement my cigarettes with what was available. Last Spring there was a disagreement with the U.S. and Indonesia about unfair trade practices. Indonesia felt that if flavored cigarettes were to be banned, that should have included menthol cigarettes which are still widely available in the United States. As a result, the U.S. lightened up its restrictions on cloves. Now you are able to purchase clove "cigars." They are skinny like the cigarettes and the packaging looks the same.

"They taste just like the cigarettes," the smoke-store guy told me. So I stocked up for my Las Vegas trip. Then I discovered the smoke-store guy had lied. These "cigars" were not like any clove cigarettes that I used to smoke. They were harsher.

I hated them but they were all I had. I noticed after smoking a few of them that they made my lips swell a bit. I started to get what looked like a cold sore right in the spot where I held it in my mouth. Still, I kept smoking them.

When I got back from Las Vegas, I had a few left. Rather than putting them in the freezer, I continued to smoke them until the packs were gone. I should have quit after I smoked the last cigar from the last pack. Did I? You know that I didn't. I went back to the store and bought two more packs. Not one, but two. Intent to smoke.

So then I went back to the old smoker standby of establishing rules. I will only smoke three a day. Broken. I will only smoke alone. Broken. I will not smoke two in a row. Broken. I felt weak. Suddenly, after twelve years of part-time smoking, I was back to being a full-timer again.

While wallowing in my weakness, I realized the problem. I used to smoke only mild clove cigarettes. They are not good for you, but they are not nearly as bad as regular cloves. I was smoking clove cigars, with a significantly higher level of nicotine. I was no longer addicted to the social aspect of smoking, I was addicted to the nicotine. And what a rush it was.

Any smoker or former smoker can tell you, there is nothing like that first cigarette (cigar) in the morning. The nicotine flushes through your body and you get light-headed. It feels really good, but if you hate yourself for smoking, it also feels really bad.

Smoking was always a cool, casual, social thing for me; with the conversion to cigars and nicotine addiction, it became something darker.

Caught, Yellow-Handed
Holly White

There are many things to learn as you are growing up. There are the basics like walking, talking, reading and writing, and learning the difference between right and wrong. Learning to do new things is good, and also learning about the bad things you shouldn't do. Smoking is one of those bad things. Even worse is getting caught doing it. Over the years I've learned several lessons to avoid getting caught, including:

1. Hiding a pack of cigarettes in your socks only works if you're wearing long pants.

2. Remember, there is always one nosy neighbor who sees everything.

3. If you get caught with a pack of cigarettes, the excuse of "they belong to a friend" only works if they're not the same brand your parents smoke.

4. When going on a family trip, never, ever, try to hide them in your parent's suitcase.

5. When in school, "NO SMOKING!" means just that - except in high school. There will always be one "smoking" bathroom that all the students congregate in. When you find it, you will probably think you won't get caught. But teachers catch on very quickly, especially if they happen to be waiting on the other side of the door and billowing clouds of smoke emerge when the door opens. If that happens, it's time to find a new bathroom.

I grew up with parents who smoked. The worst was watching my mom try to quit. The first trial/failure came when she handed me all her cigarettes, lighters and matches. Mom told me, "Do whatever you want with them," so I did. The logical thing to do was for me to smoke them myself. I really believed that she would actually quit, and I asked her over and over if she was sure. She assured me, "Yes". I really should have known better.

The first call came around 1:00 a.m. When I picked up the phone all I heard was hysterical crying, followed by silence, "I'm sorry!" and a click. By 3:00 a.m., which was the third or fourth call, the screaming and yelling from the other end was like a horror movie. I actually ended up falling out of bed at one point. Enough was enough. I managed to find the necessary clothing I needed (robe, slippers, and glasses) and was on my way to search for a store that was still open. After driving around and finding the one store that was open, I couldn't bring myself to go in. I was wearing a nightgown and robe for crying out loud! I was a mess. The only thing left to do was bring her my cigarettes. I made it to her house without a speeding ticket. She was waiting for me, at the door, nice and calm, all smiles. I never took her cigarettes again.

Mom put in many good attempts to quit. She didn't like burn marks on her clothes. During one of her on-again off-again attempts she learned that it's probably best to stick to matches or a lighter to light your cigarettes. Using a stove burner is not preferable, especially if you are fond of your hair.

We had a lot of smokers in my family, but we also had militant opponents. Like all families, we have a family member who knows everything. In our case it is an Aunt on my husband's side who always felt it necessary to make sure that everyone knew what is good and not good for them. It would be fine if it was out of concern, but it was not. There was no hiding from her, and her opinion is the only one that matters. Thanks to her, I know how to wash and put dishes away correctly, the impropriety of going without stockings when wearing a dress, and how to chew my food forty times before swallowing. But all of those paled in comparison to the NO SMOKING campaign she was constantly on.

The torment began when I joined the family thirty-five years ago. It took only a few family functions to understand why for the next thirty-five years, we would have little if any contact with her. Before leaving for one of those all-hands-on-deck family functions, my husband instructed me not smoke before or during the function. When I asked why, he told me that Aunt has a nose of a bloodhound and eyes of a hawk, and she will track you down and torment you if she smells or sees this bad habit. I listened to his warning. Unfortunately, one of her nephews did not. She was on him like the Energizer Bunny, though there was nothing cute about her. He had to endure her insufferable wrath for forty-five minutes, with her finger pointing, nose sniffing, hawk eyes. All I could think of was that I was glad that I wasn't the one caught with yellowed, nicotine fingers.

This Aunt made a lot of enemies with her non-smoking campaign and general know-it-all attitude, but the worst relationship was between her and my sister-in-law, Mary. If there was ever a skeleton in the Aunt's closet, it was Mary. Mary and the Aunt were not even on speaking terms for the last year of the Aunt's life, though they did occasionally call each other just for the pleasure of slamming down the phone in each other's ear. Little did we know that payback was planned for the most unexpected time.

After Aunt passed away, plans for the services were made. When we arrived at the wake and stood in line to say our prayers, I instantly saw the first subtle dose of payback. As I walked up to the casket, there lay Auntie, at peace. But someone had left a special present in her casket...an ashtray.

We then made our way through the row of picture boards, which were the standard nicely arranged memorial variety. I noticed that everyone was gathered around one particular picture board. That's when I noticed Mary in the back of the room, smiling. Actually Mary doesn't really smile--she cackles, kind of like a Bond villain. And she made the picture board that everyone was huddled around.

As my husband and I made our way to the board in question, there were some horrified looks on some relative's faces. Others couldn't control their laughter. Mary managed to find the worst possible pictures and saved them for this one board. One of the pictures reminded me of that lawn ornament of the lady bending over. But the coupe de grâce was the middle picture. Smack dab in the center of the collage was a picture of Auntie--our family's Militant, Know-it-All, Anti-Smoking Campaign--with a big cigarette hanging out of her mouth.

As it turns out, it's not only political candidates that have to worry about embarrassing photos coming back to haunt them. They always say keep your friends close and your enemies closer. This is probably bad advice if your enemy has a digital camera.

Holly White is a mom of five children and has always enjoyed creative writing. She would write more in this bio, but it's time for her smoke break.

An Open Letter to Christopher Davis from His Cigarettes
Chris Davis

September 28, 2012

Dear Christopher,

We're writing to you because it seems you are approaching a very important milestone in your life and we'd like to take a moment to acknowledge your accomplishment. According to our records it has been almost one full year since you smoked your last cigarette — a lovely Parliament Light enjoyed off your back deck on the evening of October 5, 2011. Congratulations! How proud you must be!

And while you're undoubtedly still busy patting yourself on the back — and for good reason! "Quitting" is hard! — we'd like to offer some anecdotal observations that might help frame your decision in the proper light going forward.

But before we do, we want to assure you that we are on your side™, and we always have been. After all, we've been your partner in the pleasure-delivery business for more than 25 years and each and every day has been an honor to serve you. And we know that if we both put forth a little effort, things could continue along that same trajectory forever. Things could be great!™

We've been through a lot together over the past twenty-five years.

Remember when we first met, in those buildings under construction in the rain? To say that we didn't "get along" at first would be putting it mildly. Candidly speaking, you were acting a little like a pussy those first couple of days, coughing and saying glib things like "oh my god, these taste like ass." But you came around and did what was best for both of us. You manned up and got the job done.

By the time the following year rolled around, we were inseparable: two cool-as-shit peas in the proverbial high-school pod. Together we were able to maintain a friendly kinship with the burnouts while solidifying our position among the gothy types. As for the fairer sex, we were simultaneously welcomed by the bad girls while provoking a healthy amount of curious approachability among the more wholesome sorts — a perfect balance of irresponsible rebellion and sophisticated charm.

But we weren't alone. Buoyed by our new friends Drugs & Alcohol®, our carefully-crafted persona was a fait accompli. Now there was nothing we couldn't do. By the time we arrived in New York City and attached ourselves to the tit of opportunity, any doubts about our painstakingly-detailed worldview constructed over the previous decade were squelched immediately. At long last, we were home.

Twenty-five years. Doesn't that mean anything to you?

When no one else was there for you, we were. When you were lonely, bored, hungover, sick, elated, drunk, sober, frantic. You name the situation, we were there. When your mom died, we were there. Through your ridiculous relationships, we were there. After you were arrested for getting in a fight with that cab driver, who was waiting inside that manila envelope with your wallet, keys and busted-up Razor phone? We were. Can anyone else make that claim? I think not.

Seriously. What do you do with your time these days? Do you ever go outside? Do you ever take a break and just think® the way we used to? Don't you know that it's unhealthy to sit in front of that computer all day? You've got to take a breather from time to time. To collect yourself. To gather your thoughts. To plan your next move.

Speaking of which, what is your next move, pal? An eternity of nothingness?

Well, I don't know what you're doing with most of your time, but I do know what you're doing with part of your time. And it's shameful.

It happened just the other day. We were with Daniel, one of our more loyal friends, sitting on a bench when he inadvertently sent a plume of smoke your way as you walked by. You remember that, in front of the Subway, lunchtime-ish? Do you remember what you did next? Don't say you don't because we know you do.

You feigned a little cough. A fake, little, pussy cough.

Seriously, if we had possessed the ability to vomit at that moment, you can rest assured that there would have been puke everywhere — on the bench, on the sidewalk, on Daniel — ev.re.where.

After all these years you've turned into that guy. The douchebag that spontaneously fakes little fucking coughs as a way of saying "please stop invading my space with your disgusting habit" because he's too scared to say it out loud like a man. You're worse now than when you were 15 years old, cold and scared in those buildings under construction. Much worse.

Obviously you're a pussy, but that's not the worst of it. The truly shameful part? You've turned into an asshole. A big, stinky asshole.

In fact, the more and more we think about it, the more we're coming to realize that maybe we don't want you back. We're not sure if there's a relationship worth saving here. After all, who needs friends like this? We have absolutely nothing in common anymore. While we're questioning authority and solving the big philosophical issues of the day, you're out getting some occasional exercise and a smoothie!

To be perfectly blunt, no one likes a quitter™. And that's just what you are (among other things, outlined in detail above).

In short, we're going to have to think about this some more. In the meantime we suggest you take a good long look at yourself in the mirror and think about who you really are. In time you might find the courage to reconsider. But we're not going to hold our breath.

With warm regards,

Your cigarettes

PS: If you want to talk about this (LIKE A MAN™) we'll be at the Quick Stop at the corner. They're open 24 hours a day. Come by anytime.

*Chris Davis runs an advertising agency in Austin, Texas called **The Swizzle Collective**. With the support of his wife and two kids, Chris was finally able to quit smoking after countless attempts. His secret? Once you quit, you can never smoke another cigarette again. Ever.*

A Heartfelt Smoking Story
Dawn Taylor

I started smoking at a young age. I was the tender, yet impressionable, age of thirteen the first time I took a drag. At that point, I was testing the waters, or rather the smoke on the water, to keep up with my friends thinking it would make me "cool" like them. I was out with a group of friends and we were supposed to be going to the 8th grade dance at my middle school. The first cigarette went along with my first beer. I didn't care much for either at the time. However I didn't succumb to the smoking habit until I was a more mature age of fifteen.

When I started the habit I would sneak smokes from my mother. I would smoke in my bedroom where I thought I wouldn't be caught. I really never was caught, but slyly given indication that my mom knew I was smoking when she gave me a candy dish and ash tray set that was from my grandmother; at least that's what she told me. Sometimes I would smoke in the bathroom where I could watch myself exhale in the mirror, mesmerized by the clouds or steady streams of smoke leaving my lungs sometimes practicing the "art" of making a smoke ring or exhaling through my mouth and immediately inhaling the expelled steams back through my nose. What a cool move! I always kept my smoking on the down low, and wasn't at the point where I was buying them for myself. Buying my own didn't come until after I graduated high school and started college. I was still living at home, but by then I was 18 and legally able to buy them so there wasn't much Mom could say.

In the early days I told myself I could quit any time I wanted. As time went on and the nicotine addiction had me fully in its grip I would exclaim to my fellow smoking friends that I would quit when a pack of cigarettes reached a dollar. Then two dollars. This declaration went on until eventually I was paying nearly five dollars a pack.

Before I knew it nearly 30 years of this addiction had gone by, 27 to be exact. That's when the day I smoked my last cigarette came. July 22, 2005. I'll never forget that day. Not because it was the day I quit for good but because it was the day I had a heart attack. Fortunately for me it was a mild one, and except for taking a handful of pills every day, I suffered no lasting ill effects from it.

The day I had the heart attack, I remember looking at the freshly opened pack of smokes on the end table when getting ready to leave for the E.R. and thinking that I didn't want them. Roughly 12 hours later, after I had been admitted to the hospital and taken to a room and wired to a heart monitor, all I could think about was the possibility of going outside for a smoke. Not a chance that was going to happen. I was wired for sound, literally! If I left the area, an alarm at the nurses station would sound, quickly revealing that I was probably up to something I shouldn't be.

At the time I was admitted, they weren't quite sure what was going on with me so they wanted to run some tests. It was a simple blood test that revealed the infarction. When the doctor told me he asked all of the usual questions. When learning that

I had been a longtime heavy smoker (two packs a day), he bluntly told me "if you don't quit they are going to kill you". That was enough for me to not look back.

A decade later, I can honestly say I haven't had a smoke in all that time; not even a drag. Sometimes I get the urge to smoke, but the urge to live quickly overtakes it. The universe willing, I'll be here for at least another couple of decades to celebrate cessation and survival.

Dawn is an Ohio native currently living smoke-free in central Ohio with her husband of 29 years. She is the loving mother of two adult daughters, mother-in-law to two wonderful sons-in-law and proud "grand moms" to a beautiful baby granddaughter.

Sandy, Interrupted.
Colleen McCauley Coughlan

I was 15 years old, and I was in the midst of a break-up phase with my best friend. Back then we would call each other "run off-ers." That's when you go off with anybody else, at the inconvenience of the friend with no other friends (me). I managed to find some new friends during this period of friend exploration--a group of girls who had a bunch of shared experiences that chronically made me feel like the third wheel. But I wasn't home, and I wasn't alone, so by default, teen code dictated that I was having fun. Besides, they liked me! They really (didn't) like me!

I don't really remember that much about these girls. Like their names, or how I met them. Or why I called them friends. They were more like the Fox and Cat from Pinocchio, who lied to him and tried to lure him to his death. These girls stole. They swore. God forbid, they SMOKED! Even though I never, ever, ever thought I would do it, they made me take my first puff off of a menthol. I felt like Sandy from the movie Grease when Rizzo peer pressured her into having a drag, and everyone laughed at her when she started choking.

Bull shit. I was not going to be the Sandy of this group.

I was determined to get a hang of smoking. I wanted to be able to do those awesome smoke bubbles that my stepdad did. Those were freaking awesome. Or that awesome French inhale like Frenchy did in *Grease*. Oh, yeah. Being a Frenchy was way cooler than being a Sandy.

The problem with my plan was my Mom. She was part American Lung Association, part blood hound, with a heaping dose of CSI. Being an only child, I was the only case on her docket, so I was pretty screwed with absolutely everything. I look back and wonder...how? HOW did you live with this woman, but still think you could get away with smoking your menthol in the windowless bathroom? But it didn't stop me from trying.

Clippity

Cloppity.

My mom wore flip-flop slippers.

Clippity CLOPPITY.

CLIPPITY CLOPPITY

The two endless flights of stairs were a good thing and a bad thing. On one hand, I had a few precious minutes of freedom to plan my Last Will and Testament. On the other, it was an awful long time to feel Jaws' shark fin circling around me.

I honestly can't remember if I was scared, or if I thought I had gotten rid of the smell. In the end, it didn't matter. I have a remarkable knack for self-sabotage, and Mom smelled a bad decision on me before I even made it. I ended up grounded for like a million years and my new best friends never spoke to me again.

But I still kept smoking. I smoked for 20 years, on and off, up until my midlife surprise pregnancy. That pregnancy's delightful side effect was nausea, exasperated by the smell of smoke, thus ending my decades-long affair. Whenever I see the price of cigarettes, I'm very glad I quit. Sure babies are more expensive, but there is far more return on investment. Not to mention, payback.

If anyone is interested in getting me a Christmas present this year, at the top of my list is a pair of flip-flop slippers.

Colleen McCauley Coughlan would love to be sponsored by Phillip Morris and take her comedy routine out on the road to venues filled with people who still smoke indoors.

This is Not a Cigarette
Denise Robichau

I've imagined myself in black and white stills and moving motion pictures. A smoke ring drifts in the space just outside where my eyes focus and smoke rushes up my nose, the perfect French inhale.

Except, smoking is yet another activity in which any illusion of cool reserve, hipness, insouciance is betrayed. I look decidedly awkward and at risk of lighting things on fire.

I always wanted to be a smoker. Smoking is my sixth grade crush, Greg Maharis, with a pack of Marlboros in his shirt pocket. Intentionally unfazed, he flaunted his vice under the disapproving looks of any and all adults. I think inhaling might have been secondary to his having the pack on hand, a badge of dishonor.

Twice in my life, I have approached joining the club with vigor and resolve.

In college, I banged away on my typewriter, the relic of old-timey writing. Near my right elbow, two fingers of Jack Daniels. In front of my left hand a stolen ashtray and a Camel.

It seemed like a natural fit to the wild life I had assumed. I shared with an older student and chain smoker a crusty, off-campus apartment, the only place I ever cohabited with roaches. Unlike the old cigarette ad, I'd rather switch than fight, so I adopted my roommate's vice rather than ask her to step into an Upstate New York winter and smoke outside. We settled into the dark space in a sketchy neighborhood and imagined ourselves reckless outsiders to the safety and clean air of dormitories.

Straight bourbon and unfiltered cigarettes were the ingredients I imagined my muse craved. After all, I was a student journalist, imagining a future of hardbitten late nights courting deadlines with important truths, while penning my own novel alone in a garret. This place, this dilapidated apartment,m was my debut.

Honestly, bourbon and smoke make me sputter. My smoker's squint is more cross eyed than steely. I tear. My nose twitches or runs. In the cold light of reality, I get a little nauseous with either the rush of nicotine or the heat of neat bourbon landing in the pit of my stomach. Together, the chemical reaction is volatile.

I kept the props with my typewriter, though. The pack of Camels stayed at ready reach, even as they became stale and started to spontaneously disintegrate. The Jack went down much easier with ice and Coke.

For many years afterwards, I flirted with cigarettes.

They were often there on a communal table among beer glasses or bottles and the occasional joint. The quintessential late night companion to rambling discussions, loud bands, hook ups and yelling into friends' ears at pubs and bars. Cigarettes were the catalyst for initiating conversations in dark places and low corners. "Hey, can I bum a smoke?"

I stayed mostly smokeless in my 30s. While various friends and I still gathered, palates and wallets changed. With better wines and finer dinners the communal smokes were stowed away by the smokers in deference to changing laws.

Late in my 30s, early in my 40s, I tried to re-cultivate the habit lost with my old typewriter.

The occasion was an almost crippling insomnia born from aspiring to be a stand up comic while mourning the death of my mother. My brain just refused to sleep, and I opted for staying night after night until closing at any and every bar with a microphone and stage time.

Miraculously, my body and mind agreed that I was in no state to become a full-blown alcoholic. When I couldn't drink any more, I smoked.

Back outside, where I would walk miles home to fill my lungs with sobering fresh, night air, I would feel purged from the vices inside a bar.

The only people willing to stay up along side me and ponder the pointlessness of doing so, and who had the stamina, were a couple I knew drenched in conspiracy theories. Their compulsion to talk about the government, coverups, 9/11, the occult, science, the afterlife, life as we thought we knew it, the

Trilateral Commission, Diet Coke, pharmaceutical companies, NATO and the UN, dovetailed nicely with my inability to sleep.

They didn't smoke. They didn't particularly care for smoking. Big Tobacco is indeed a real conspiracy with a nefarious history of marketing poisons for billions of dollars. At least on that one we agreed, even as I lit another cigarette.

It became a ritual that reached from days to months and then almost a year. The male of the conspiracy couple and I would each have our five to ten minutes of time on stage at a comedy club, settle in the back and wait out the show. I nursed a light beer and he and his wife drank whatever beverage was not currently deemed unsafe by the internets.

Eventually, the house lights would go up, the erstwhile stage would revert to a backdrop for a conventional bar. I started with "borrowing" from friends or buying loosies, although I graduated to buying my own cigarette packs, switching brands with no loyalty or particular reason.

The conspiracy couple comforted me with their certain knowledge that my mom and I will meet again. They shared names of local mediums, who could arrange a conversation. They explained that even for non-Catholics, the repetition of the rosary comforts the dead and is able to penetrate to the hearts of dead loved ones. Alongside nicotine and beer I soaked in their beliefs, wishing for a glimmer of truth.

I was an emotional wreck. My mother's death was a heavy weight. I worried over her loss and whether I had done enough before she was gone. I grieved. I went from crying to numbness to handing the usual business. Our family survived the usual dance with the arguments and closeness and sharing and squabbles of all siblings.

I knew that I had almost stopped sleeping. But, for all outward appearances I was doing OK.

Her absence created an imbalance in my life. I had been in the habit of weekly shopping and running errands with and for her over years. It was our routine. My solo routine was now late nights, knowing there would be no Sunday phone call recriminations from my mother.

I never smoked in the daylight. I seldom smoked at home. I never looked forward to cigarettes or craved them.

Maybe I'm the lucky few impervious to nicotine's addictive nature.

But, they were there for me. Cigarettes gave my hands something to do, when my mind couldn't process waves of intense emotion. Smoking was a simple fatalistic act. It had its own peculiar joy. It was also a connection to the now-gone woman who had herself secretly smoked away from the eyes of the five children she raised.

With cigarette poised between my fingers, I was in control of at least one thing for a few passing minutes.

And, then I stopped. The last pack was empty, and I stayed home. I slept the night. I never even said goodbye to the sweet, burning lover that had sustained me stick by stick until it was time to move on.

Leaving roots, family and some unclaimed junk in New England, Denise Robichau now lives on the coast in the San Francisco Bay area, occasionally turning up at open mikes, comedy showcases and storytelling events. Her newest form of procrastination from updating her weblog or photo gallery at http://dee-rob.com or working on an unfinished memoir, "Burying My Mom in Leopard Print Undies," is unsuccessfully crab fishing on the local pier or beach while playing games on her iPhone.

Ah...Good Times
Julia Wagner

If I'd given any thought as to what kind of an addict to become, I think I would have chosen sex addict; at least there is a naughty thrill that accompanies the admission. Or... cocaine addict, which would have allowed me to be far more productive, I am sure. But no, nicotine addict is what I ended up with, and it truly can become an addiction, particularly for a person whose vocabulary doesn't include the word moderation.

I started smoking when I was a teenager. One of a slew of stupid decisions, this one I think I made because my brother smoked and big brothers are cool. I started sneaking half smoked cigarettes of my grandma's (yuck). As long as breath mints were available, I was able to keep this on the down-low – who is going to smell the smoke of one more cigarette in an apartment that reeked already?

Smoking out in public resulted in a whole new level of risk. Getting them wasn't the problem (there were cigarette machines back in the 80's); the problem was keeping it a secret. One day outside during high school lunch I waved at a friend of my mother's who was driving by, totally forgetting that I had a smoke in my hand. Another time I was lighting a cigarette and set a good bit of my hair on fire. I can't remember what excuse I used for that one.

At any rate, onesie-twosie became a pack a day habit at some point in my 20's. I was amassing a vast quantity of anti-tobacco literature sent thoughtfully by my mother, who at this point had figured the whole thing out. And, the habit was not only getting expensive, but dangerous. Early one morning, my husband stepped onto the front porch and was met by the smell of smoke. I'd put my last evening cigarette out in the mulch and had, well, sort of set it on fire. In my mind, I'd put the cigarette out in dirt.... his response was "honey, mulch is wood, wood is flammable!" Oops.

There came a time in my late 30's when I decided that I needed to quit. I'd quit once for two months, and had tried a smoking cessation drug (a disaster) and hypnosis (relaxing, but useless) and nothing had ever worked. This time would be different, I thought. I smoked my last cigarette and threw out the empty pack, with a vow not to buy any more.

That was almost 4 years ago, and looking back, I'm not sure I would have made the same decision. Hands down one of the top five worst weekends of my life.

My last cigarette was in the afternoon on a Friday, and by Saturday midday, I'd pretty much flown off the handle. I was doing dishes and my husband (who'd not been clued into the whole quitting thing) said something to me. I have no idea what he said, but several seconds later, I had a two-handed grip on a cookie sheet, and was slamming it as hard as I could onto the kitchen counter. Angry tears commenced...

At some point during that day, he got smart and left me to my hysterics. Saturday night at about 1 AM found me on a busy street corner, about two blocks from a gas station, "Camel" blinking on and off in the window, on foot and in tears. Did I mention it was December? I spent over an hour on that street corner, pacing and crying and clutching the $5 bill I'd brought with me. I made it through that night without a cigarette, but it was by the skin of my teeth. Four years later and I still fight the cravings.

So, words of wisdom to anyone that plans the "cold turkey" method of quitting (anything) - remove sharp objects and avoid alcohol if possible. Then settle in for a very looonnngggg couple of days.

Julia lives with her non-smoking husband, non-smoking dog and non-smoking cat in Columbus, Ohio where her life's ambition is to become a roadside carnival performer and grow her own vegetables.

Cough and Gag, Give Me Another
Teresa Whitaker

I started smoking a million years ago. Okay, so
not that long ago, but it has been 35 plus years. My
first cigarette was not behind the barn or in some
alleyway; it was in the girl's bathroom at middle
school. I was 11 years old. I still remember trying not
to cough and gag. The cool kids were smoking like
pros and I so wanted to be cool. The bathroom,
although technically a girl's room, was usually
packed with both boys and girls, smoke billowing
out the only window. There was an element of
engaging in the forbidden, of breaking the rules.
Actually, I never understood how we were never
caught. The only possible explanation was it was
another time, when smoking really was not
considered a bad thing and so the teachers and
school administration did nothing about it. We kids,
however, felt like we were really something,
breaking the rules and getting away with it. Real
badasses, in today's vernacular.

I continued to smoke, where and when I could. Stealing cigarettes from other people and if I was lucky finding someone with a pack who would share. I had a little old lady who lived in my neighborhood that had no problem giving me cigarettes, which I carefully stored in my socks. Did not want to break them. When you are begging, borrowing and stealing smokes, a broken cigarette was the worst!

As I got a bit older and entered high school, it was easier to get cigarettes. A pack of cigarettes cost 55 cents. Oh, sounds so cheap now, but getting 55 cents together when you are 13 or 14 years old wasn't all that easy. When I did manage to scrape the money together, off to the local liquor store I would go. All the kids knew which liquor store would sell you cigarettes. I would buy my pack, which could last me two weeks. Again, the stigma of smoking that is prevalent today was non-existent back then. Our high school even had a smoking area, where, again, all the cool kids hung out. Yes, I was finally a cool kid. At least I was when I was in the smoking area.

I was in my 30's before the thought of quitting smoking even entered my mind. I had a few bouts with a collapsed lung. It is a genetic thing and not directly related to smoking, but I was advised to quit as the collapse and the subsequent operation left scar tissue. The scar tissue diminished lung capacity and they told me that my lungs were quite black. So I did quit. For a day or two. Then something would happen. I would get angry, sad, a party would happen, I would be bored, whatever and I would smoke again. Thus began my never-ending journey to quit.

I have spent many years trying to quit. The longest time I have quit was a year. That time I chewed the gum, I used the drugs and I went to Disneyland for a week. That helped me get through the first week. Then my niece was diagnosed with leukemia and while being treated came down with acute respiratory distress syndrome (ARDS). She was not expected to live. She was only 6. As I sat with my sister, crying, completely torn, I grabbed one of her smokes. It helped to calm. Damn if it wasn't like I never quit. And that nicotine worked its magic. I was calmer and better able to get my sister through the time of crisis (I am happy to say my niece made it through as well).

I have tried many ways to quit. I have used the patch, the gum, lozenges, hypnosis, cold turkey, acupuncture, meditation, clove cigarettes, switching brands, switching to cigars, cutting back, and probably some I have forgotten. I have tried to lay down rules: Only smoking after meals, before or after work, never smoking around the kids, not smoking in the car, only smoking in the car, never smoking in public or only smoking in public. I could go on but you get the picture. The worst is that I could never follow my own rules. No method seems to work. So, I devour all literature on quitting smoking, poring over the pamphlets, the self-help books, the suggestions from my doctor. They all seem to be written by people who have never smoked. Substituting carrots, indeed. Talking a walk. Chewing on a toothpick. Nope, they have not smoked or they would know that the problem is in my head.

In my head is where I get messed up. I am not happy smoking. I have emphysema, a moderate case, and if I quit I will live for many years to come. So that should be motivation enough, right? Wrong. People who do not smoke don't get it. Most mean well, but if I could "just quit" I would have a long time ago. If thinking of all the reasons to quit were enough, I would have already quit. Thinking of all the money I would save doesn't do it.

I truly wish there was a magic wand. I do. There isn't. I am stuck with making plans and scheming on how to quit. Every day. And then feeling like a loser because I don't. I don't quit. I don't follow my own plans. My head tells me when I have that first cigarette, well you screwed up today, might as well smoke. And I agree with my head only to feel like I have disappointed everyone, including myself. Laying in bed feeling like a hopeless case. Every morning waking up resolved to do better. My life has become a never-ending obsession with quitting the cigarettes and so far, the cigarettes are winning. I do have another quit date of June 16. This time, I am taking a class provided by my doctor. It is an all-day affair. I want it to work. I need it to work. I just have to convince my head.

Teresa Whitaker, 49 year old mother and wife is also an author and blogger. After smoking for over 35 years, Teresa Whitaker is finally going to quit. Again. She thinks. She is currently trying to quit for the umpteenth time and is chronicling her journey in a blog, aptly name "theblogofteresa". Having previously written for children, Teresa is now writing for the grownups of the world. She currently resides in the California Bay Area with her man and her insane cat, where she spends her days writing and living happily ever after.

Dear Ciggy
Nina Pelletier

Dear Ciggy,

A "Dear John" letter was never the way I expected to end things. But let's face it, one look at you and I'd lose any and all determination to butt out our affair.

"An Affair", that's an interesting term to use for a 20 year relationship. I remember when we first met, how I watched you and swore I would never succumb to your seductions. You were the leader of the pack, and I was the good girl on the sidelines bad talking your wicked ways to anyone whose lips you touched. And let's be honest, you touched a lot of lips.

But in a moment of weakness, there you were, dangling your charms in front of me, promising me comfort and acceptance. Just like that, the match of love was struck and the fire burned so brightly that I was beyond smitten with you. Through the filter of girlhood crush, I was oblivious to the blue-grey cloud of death that hovered above our heads.

How could I see it beyond your fierce devotion to my needs? You. You were the one that was always there. When my dad died, you were there. When I celebrated my graduation, you were there. When I cried alone in the night, you were there. When I was bored, when I was lonely, when I needed a distraction or a break, you were there. In every moment of want and need, you never failed to offer my hand your comfort.

Oh sure, you've played around, but I've been loyal through and through. Though I've seen you with others, I felt I understood the real you better than anyone else could. As I watched those stronger than me abandon you, I convinced myself they didn't love you as much as I do, they didn't understand your fire. I was the fool.

I didn't see how much you were hurting me. I mistook you always being there for me as devotion, the feeling of bliss when I breathed you in as love, the hunger for you when I couldn't have you as need. In truth, you weren't devoted; you stalked me. The feeling of bliss was a mind trick you pulled on me like a chemical version of a magician's smokescreen. The hunger, oh, the hunger that was merely an addiction. Our time together was the ultimate example of an abusive relationship, where one is so blind they can't even see the destruction right before their eyes.

Yet, alas Ciggy, my darling, even as I write how bad you are for me, I crave your full-flavored kisses even now. Please stay away and let me throw the ashes of our cancerous love to the wind.

No longer yours truly,
X. Smoker

P.S.

The match of love was struck and the fire burned so brightly that I sat smitten, oblivious to the blue-grey cloud of death that hovered above our heads.

Filter

Pack

Carton

Burn

Matches

Lighter

Flick

Ashes

Butt

Smoke

Cancerous

Nina Pelletier is a full-time writer who lives in Ontario, Canada. She is the creator of the Prompt-and-Share and the co-creator and editor of "Letters to my Ten-Year-Old Self". When she's not prompting, editing, providing feedback, reading, blogging or writing, she can be found playing with her canine companion, Princess Trixie.

The Smoking Room
Del Gaddie

I've never been a smoker - I never understood what made it so cool to my friends.

Well, that's not really true – we watched the same movies growing up. I guess watching Clint Eastwood in a spaghetti western has an effect on some people more than others.

I can't say I understand the appeal, either. Once, I watched a friend smoke dried catnip in an attempt to get his cigarette fix. As you can imagine, it didn't work. I think I hurt myself laughing while he hacked and gagged in absolute failure.

I have a theory – I think that a smoker can always tell if a nonsmoker is vehemently opposed to smoking. It always seems that the smoke clouds get thicker and the griping gets a little louder. To be fair, though, I imagine that nonsmokers think that smokers secretly hate them for their piety.

I am one of those people who do a private little celebration dance when a city passes another 'no smoking' ordinance. Of course, the downside is that now I have to hold my breath walking into any large building – smokers stand like war-worn sentries in a fog of cigarette smoke. I try not to make eye contact. I can feel their nicotine-addled gaze reading my thoughts. They can tell I don't like smelling like an ashtray when I walk into the building. Sometimes, a smoker will follow me into the building and ride up the same elevator. Is this coincidental? Probably – but my sense of conspiracy remains elevated.

I'm sure that this is a really unfair association, but I think that hoarders and smokers are all secret Libertarians. They both seem to have a highly focused sense of how what they do is a protected right, regardless of the impact to others.

As I've said – I've never been a smoker. I'm pretty sure I get the 'non-smoker stare' when I'm holding my breath to get into the office tower.

I used to work at a hospital in the Environmental Services department. I've always liked that term – Environmental Services – it always had a better ring than 'custodial engineer' or janitor.

In our hospital we had a smoking room. It was a small, glass-walled room that patients and hospital guests could use to catch a quick smoke and commune with each other. Whenever I went inside to empty the ashtrays, the banter always seemed to be the same. Conversations went from complaining about the price of a carton of cigarettes to the lack of smoking accommodations. Often, there was a comment or two about the government violating of the rights of smokers.

One day, I was assigned to close and scrub the smoking room from top to bottom – a 'voluntary' assignment. I was a relatively new employee to the hospital, and I didn't really see what the big deal was. I volunteered in order to avoid having to do trash duty all evening. At the time, it didn't occur to me that none of the smokers on the crew volunteered.

So my evening began. I grabbed a couple of buckets of really hot water, some caustic smelling cleanser, a large quantity of washcloths, and set to work. The room was probably 10x20ft, with hard benches around the entire room. There was a large sectioned window that allowed the smokers to watch hospital traffic go by, and an exhaust fan that served as the room's air conditioning and ventilation. The walls were lined with that yellowish plastic covering you often see in the back of a fast food restaurant. I have to admit that I was completely unprepared for the evening. I also understood why the smokers avoided the assignment.

As I scrubbed the walls down, I was amazed to see that the plastic wall covering in the room was actually a bright white color. Great streaks of brownish-yellow ichor dripped from the walls like an industrial horror movie. A year's worth of cigarette residue had stained and collected on the walls and furniture. As I scrubbed, great puddles of foamy brown ick covered the floor. I had to change my water buckets more than a few times in order to make progress. It took three full passes scrubbing every surface to remove the smoking residue.

As I scrubbed the film off the glass, I could see the glares of the regular smokers boring through the haze. It was a particularly humid evening, and the smoking room was relatively cooler than the sidewalk outside. There were a few patients with IV carts passing dirty glances for the inconvenience.

As the ceiling was also coated with the smoke residue, I would be required to scrub it as well. As I cleaned, soapy brown water began to drip in my hair, on my clothes, and onto my skin. To say I was disgusted would be an epic understatement.

There was a nasty side effect to cleaning the room. I wasn't in a position to change my clothes as I cleaned, so the residue remained on my clothes leaching into my skin. I began to feel lightheaded and a bit euphoric as I continued working. As the evening wore on, both sensations combined to an odd sense of nausea- something like riding a rollercoaster with a migraine. Suffice to say the nausea lasted longer than the lightheaded euphoria.

A whole eight hours later, the room was glistening white. The windows were clear and inviting – it was possible to see quite a bit later in the evening with the haze removed. The floors were scrubbed, and all evidence of the room's functionality had been cleaned. As I moved my equipment out of the room, the smokers filed passed me. A few of the older gentlemen grunted as they passed, happy that the inconvenience had finally ended.

I left for the evening smelling of soap and nicotine. I felt as if I left a vapor cloud of tar and nicotine in my wake. My pores felt clogged with the brown ichor that dripped from the walls and ceiling. As I walked past the smoking room on my way to my car, I could see a half dozen smokers in the room, all working hard on getting the new layer of residue back on the walls. The room was deep cleaned once a year. I knew I would not be volunteering again for that detail under any circumstances.

As experiences go, I have to rate cleaning that room as one of the most disgusting. I understand now why the smokers on the crew avoided the assignment – I'm guessing one of two reasons. Either the task is so monumental that they would rather not do it (even if they would be allowed to smoke on the job), or the consequences of smoking hit a little too close to home in there. I can't be sure.

Del Gaddie is a non-smoker in the central Ohio area. He is happily married with two little non-smokers and a cat who may be 'a bit witchy.' When Del is not sitting in front of a PC writing web programs, he engages in photographing 'Cute Macabre'. To get a better understanding of Cute Macabre, you are invited to visit Del at www.braains.com

How I Quit Smoking through Hypnosis
David Horning

In March of 1980, I was living on the east coast, but had received a transfer and was scheduled to move to the San Francisco Bay area the following month. At the time, I was a casual smoker; I didn't smoke at work ... only when drinking, or playing cards with friends. I often bought cigarettes at a bar, but just as often politely inquired from strangers if I could "borrow" one of theirs. Their frequent graciousness beguiled me into believing that this was acceptable behavior; however, my cousin, Martha, suggested otherwise.

When last in Martha's company, we were having cocktails with relatives, and someone asked what brand I smoked. Suddenly, Martha blurted out, "Dave smokes OPCs - Other People's Cigarettes". The burst of laughter surprised me into the realization that the bumming of cigarettes was indeed obnoxious and socially reprehensible. Thus,

I had a choice to make: buy a carton of my own cigarettes or ... quit smoking.

The next week was one of procrastination. On Friday night, while visiting a local mall, I encountered a hypnotist hired to entertain the shoppers. He had assembled ten volunteers, and as I watched, he told them to relax, close their eyes, and count backward from 100. The volunteers stood in front of the onlookers with their eyes closed. They were hypnotized.

The hypnotist's first instruction was that the sounds they were hearing from the audience were the sounds of waves crashing on the beach. In fact, they were at the beach and could feel the ocean breeze.

Next, he announced that he had bought them each an ice cream cone. He told them that they were going to be part of an ice cream cone eating contest. The winner would get a ten dollar prize, but there were rules ... no biting the ice cream ... licking only. On the count of three, all ten stuck out their tongues and began lapping furiously at the air in a frenetic yet practiced manner. The audience convulsed with laughter; yet, all ten continued unabashedly in their pursuit of the prize.

Suddenly, the hypnotist declared the contest was over and that everyone had tied. All would receive the prize. He told them he was going to give them each a $10 bill, but they had to hide it in a secure place as there were reports of pickpockets nearby. As he gave them each the imaginary money, they quickly stuffed it in a secure place. (Yes, all the women stuffed it in their bras.) Remarkably, the laughter of the audience did not awaken any of the volunteers.

Suddenly, the hypnotist paused. He announced that he believed one of the volunteers to be under the age of 18. As he brought her out of hypnosis, he informed her that she would remember everything that had just happened. As she slowly opened her eyes, she immediately put her hand to her mouth and began gasping with red-faced embarrassment. She had indeed remembered. Her friends were laughing with her as they left to re-live the event.

Then, the hypnotist announced that he would demonstrate a post-hypnotic suggestion. He singled out one of the volunteers, and brought her forward. While her eyes were still closed, he gave her a cookie. He told her that she would find the cookie delicious, but if he touched her right shoulder, the cookie would then taste like burnt rubber. He told her to open her eyes and she did. Was she still under his spell??

She began eating the cookie and she was enjoying it. Then, he put his hand on her right shoulder and triggered the post-hypnotic suggestion. She immediately began to gag and spit the cookie bits onto the floor. As he removed his hand from her shoulder, he told her that she had gotten a bad cookie, but assured her that the next cookie would be good. As the cruel episode repeated itself, our uproarious laughter still did not awaken any of the volunteers.

Then, the hypnotist proclaimed that the show was over. He began bringing the volunteers out of hypnosis, and declared that they would remember nothing. As the participants opened their eyes, their friends from the audience gathered around them. As predicted, none of the volunteers remembered anything! They displayed a look of disbelief as their friends described what had happened. I was impressed.

The hypnotist then announced that on the next night he was going to hold a session for smokers who wanted to quit, and that it would it would only cost $25. I was sold.

When I returned the next evening, I joined a group of four others who were there for this next session. After taking our payments, the hypnotist instructed us to light up and smoke. We sat on chairs in an empty storefront and enjoyed our cigarettes. The hypnotist continued by explaining the entire program to us. We would be put under hypnosis. During the first part of the session, he would allow us to remember the unfolding events, but not the second part. He explained the process as trying to break the link between seeing a cigarette and wanting one. He explained the psychology of advertising ... to trigger a desire upon receiving visual stimulus. He further explained that it was his goal to substitute desire with revulsion. He discussed one of his childhood experiences when he had viewed the red rings of the kitchen range, but had not perceive the danger. He described in detail how he had put his own hand on the bright red rings of the range and felt the pain; this experience was seared in his brain. This visual stimulus of red glowing rings would forever discomfort him.

The hypnotist explained that he was going to create a similar scar upon our brains. And, that hereafter, we would view cigarettes as he viewed red glowing rings. He also explained that he was NOT going to stop us from smoking - just from smoking the next cigarette. He told us to extinguish our cigarettes and declared that wc had just smoked our last one. Then, he told us to close our eyes and count backwards; I fell helplessly under his spell.

I remember the first part of the session. The initial step was to picture ourselves in a tranquil scene beside a babbling brook. He asked us to throw our cigarettes, one by one, into these waters. As we cast each cigarette away, he asked us to associate each cigarette with a letter from that word. He quietly suggested "C for Cancer", and moved slowly yet deliberately to the last letter ... "E for Emphysema". When our last cigarette was tossed away, the pack was also discarded into the brook.

In the next exercise, we were told to picture ourselves fishing on a beach. Then ... we became fish as the cigarettes became bait on a large and jagged hook. We pictured ourselves being caught by this hook and felt the pain of the hook in our lip as we were reeled in.

That was the last thing I remembered. The second half of the session still remains a mystery. Then, as the session ended, we were told to open our eyes.

It worked. I haven't smoked a cigarette since that moment. However, I am concerned that the hypnotist ... somewhere deep in the recesses of my brain ... has planted a post-hypnotic suggestion. So, if you are ever at a party or a bar, and you see someone take an initial drag on a cigarette, and then begin screaming in pain while trying to remove an imaginary hook from their lip ... hey, come over and say hello.

Dave grew up in Columbus, Ohio as a son of a smoker of Tareyton cigarettes ... his father believed in that brand's logo: "I'd rather fight than switch." Dave showed no such brand loyalty and was willing to smoke any brand of someone else's cigarette.

Up in Smoke
Jennifer Packard

To date a smoker or not to date a smoker...that is the question. Deciding to allow smoking to be included (or excluded) on your dating checklist is a bigger deal than it seems. It can range anywhere from deal breaker to acceptable depending on the person, or with some people, depending on at different times in their lives. Most people I've known or have talked to throughout the years tend to be pretty black and white about this, usually meaning an 'Absolute no' for non- smokers, or a 'That's okay because I smoke myself' for smokers. What I've found in my own life is that my acceptability of a partner smoking changed as I got older and the dating world was somewhat harder to navigate, then later making a sort of U-turn and going back to my original opinion. This article of course is only from my point of view and life only, everyone has their own.

When I was in my twenties and had just broken into the dating world (yes I was a late bloomer with pretty much everything), I just threw myself in blind and the first guy I had a relationship with turned out to be a smoker and I didn't care. Now no one in my family smoked, but I was so excited and wrongly infatuated with my first boyfriend, that I ignored him lighting up like a toddler ignores looking both ways for cars on a busy road. I was all enveloped and it didn't matter. As we went out dancing, to parties or the movies, he (we'll call him 'C' for privacy sake) would light up to and from wherever we were headed. I can't remember how much he smoked at the start or if he hid it and smoked more the more comfortable we got, but looking back I truly can't believe how much he smoked. A couple people in his family were already diagnosed with emphysema, and he continued to smoke like a chimney. It was then that I realized the environmental connection, and how truly difficult an addiction it was. I do remember virtually holding my breath for the first six months we were dating every time we kissed, and due to the insanity of a first time infatuation, I never said a word. I never thought I could or should. How I didn't pass out from holding my breath that first year, I'll never know. But towards the end when 'C' finally asked why I never opened my mouth all the way I had to confess. "It's your breath. All I taste is smoke". I wanted to say "It's like kissing an ashtray" but I couldn't, even though he wasn't the kindest person to me anyway. I must emphasize this was not the reason we broke up, but having done so, I swore I would never date another smoker and I didn't for the better part of the next eighteen years.

Then I met a writer just like me. Looking back, a lot of the guys I dated (or was attracted to) were either artists or writers due to our common interests drawing us together in the same circles. That first boyfriend I told you about, a would-be accountant, was not one, but for most of my dating years it was artists or writers I was drawn to. I'm tempted to say that maybe smoking was a trait associated with them, since they tended to be more free and edgy types, but even of this I'm still not sure. This new writer (we can call him 'Jeff' because I've never actually dated a Jeff) was an attractive and smart wordsmith with piercing blue eyes who admitted upfront that he did have a cigarette every once in a while. Because of our interests and attraction, (and my desire to find 'the one') I figured I'd let it slide. Having lived a lot more of life now and having navigated through my own food addiction lasting for a good ten years, I could appreciate having one and how difficult it was to finally overcome it. A food addiction of any kind doesn't physically affect other people around those that have it though, unlike smoking. I wanted to see past it; to ignore it and just focus on 'Jeff'. In the end he wasn't the right person and the relationship was short lived, I have to say in large part due to how much he hid the actual size of his habit and the misrepresentation of it. Had I known in the beginning, I could have formed an opinion more quickly, but Jeff's description of his addiction could be compared to someone describing a tiny hole in their sweater, then when you finally see it, realizing the hole is actually the size of the Grand Canyon. One hot summer day, Jeff decided to reveal exactly how much he smoked, and it was like an every -now – and- then smoker turning into Sean Penn right before my eyes. (and nothing against Sean Penn because we all know he's the best!) But throughout the course of our date, Jeff lit up so much that I'm surprised the reeds lining the beach we were walking didn't catch fire. I was astounded at the amount, but more astounded by how much he hid it. When I asked him about trying to quit, his response was 'I can't do that and start a new relationship' and that was that. This of course I understood and respected. I guess the size of his addiction was just too big.

In any recent dating (and in between the necessary breaks we take) along with other life events happening, I tried to stay away from smokers. But as we age, even though smoking is a deal breaker for most people, we also realize that the people we date can be all wrong for us for many ways, not just smoking. Womanizing and commitment phobia abound in the dating ocean, and after one too many tastes of this sort of thing, it made me want to sit back down at the negotiating table with smoking and see if we can come up with some sort of a deal. I am sitting down with it now as I currently date a really cool, kind, funny (and yes, creative and artistic) man of my own age who is neither a womanizer nor commitment- phobe. He too didn't want to admit how much he smoked in the beginning, but it's not as bad as the other situations. After five months of a very good, but still young relationship, there are many things I truly respect and admire about this man. We have fun together and many common interests, so it is now that find myself trying to ignore the fact that I don't want to get as close to him as I could in the movie theater, that I can smell smoke on his clothes which then gets on mine, that it's in my hair when I leave his house and I have to take a shower, and yes, unfortunately I am back to holding my breath again. It is at this point in the article that I want to shout

"Help" to anyone who will listen. What should I do?
I so respect what smokers have to go through, how
they become addicted, and the unimaginable
willpower it must take to quit. But then there's my
sense of smell, taste and lifestyle too. I guess this is
the age old dilemma of 'To date a smoker or not to
date a smoker.'

*Jennifer Packard is a Rhode Island based writer
who has a few short stories published, one in 'Woe
of the Road' entitled 'Ditched'. She is turning her
award winning sci fi short story 'Reciprocity' into a
screenplay. In her spare time she enjoys movies,
family and friends, photography, and her cat
Koobie (the star of a lot of her pictures).*

Little Miss Surgeon General
Kyle Therese Cranston

"If you don't quit smoking, you're going to get cancer and die," I said to one of my aunts as I crossed my arms defiantly over my chest and narrowed my eyes.

I believe it was a sunny afternoon, and we were barbecuing in the backyard. All of my cousins were running around playing freeze tag, swinging on swings, and other activities parents encourage their children to participate in so they will be worn-out by bedtime. But, not me. No, I wasn't playing; I was condemning. I was lecturing. I was being an all-around pain in the ass.

My aunt just rolled her eyes at me and kept puffing away. She might've even yelled for my mom to come and get her annoying, know-it-all daughter the hell away from her. I can only speculate about this as I was only five at the time.

Yes, I was a five-year-old who felt the need to form an anti-smoking crusade. Keep in mind that this was well before all those Truth campaign commercials featuring an obscene amount of black body bags and creepy old people talking out of voice boxes hit the TV waves. To this day I have no idea where my hatred of smoking stems from and why at such an early age, I was so anti-cigarette. It may have been the mid 80s and I may have only been a child, but I was on a mission—a mission to rid the world of smokers through the power of my words, no matter how annoying they were.

And, I didn't just lecture my smoking relatives, but I also used my childlike "getting my own way" power of the silent treatment to punish my mom anytime she lit up. She only smoked once in a great while, just when she was hanging out in her sister's backyard while my brother and I horsed around with our cousins. But, the minute she lit up, I ran to her side, ranted and raved about how she was killing herself, and then refused to talk to her for hours after. Luckily, my dad hated smoke just as much as I did, so it wasn't a habitual occurrence. I think he actually found my judgmental shenanigans amusing. Plus, it saved him from having to be the bad guy.

I remember lecturing my grandpa about his smoking habit because frankly, I loved the guy and wanted him to be around for a long time. He eventually quit, but not because of his strong-willed granddaughter's words of wisdom. The man got mad at the tobacco industry for constantly raising the price of cigarettes and quit cold turkey out of spite. I considered writing them a thank-you letter. Yay for capitalistic greed!

But, I didn't care how annoyed people got with me and my stop-smoking lectures. Cigarettes were public enemy number one to me, and they still are today.

Now, I know I sound like a total brat, but my Judge Judy act really did come from a place of love. I honestly believed my loved ones faced an early, cancer-ridden death. But, was it my place to warn them about the dangers of smoking? Probably not.

Now that I'm in my 30s, I'm even more against smoking than ever, but I'm also well aware that my

Little Miss Surgeon General act didn't work then, and it won't work now. In fact, instead of eye rolls, I now face the risk of getting bitch slapped, which frankly doesn't sound like fun.

So, needless to say, I've taken it down a notch. I now take a more passive-aggressive approach to demonstrate my strong hatred of smoking. For instance, instead of wagging my finger at a smoker who lights up near me, I now cough loudly enough to resemble a TB patient. Whether they scurry away from me because they think I have a contagious lung disease or because they are picking up on my "get your second-hand smoke away from my precious lungs" vibe, I'm not entirely sure. But, it works either way, so I'll take it. I also automatically hold my breath whenever I pass by a smoker, which proved to be a problem when I went to Las Vegas for a long weekend since I can only hold my breath for like 30 seconds before feeling like I'm going to suffocate.

And since I hate smoking, I obviously refuse to date a smoker either. In fact, that's the first thing I scan on a guy's online dating profile. The few times smokers have contacted me on OkCupid, I coldly stated via email that I don't date smokers...ever. I even once had the gall to ask a guy who emailed me about possibly meeting up why he smoked. I believe my exact words were: "Why the hell do you smoke anyway? It's so 1999."

Seriously smokers, I don't get it. What's so great about inhaling carcinogenic tar? What's so great about your fingernails turning yellow? What's so great about mossy teeth and a constant hacking cough? I understand addictions and know firsthand they aren't easy to kick. I mean, I had a hell of a time giving up coffee rolls from Dunkin Donuts, so I know how hard it is. What I don't get is why you start smoking to begin with.

Oh well, it's a free country, so people say, so I guess I should shut my mouth and let all you smokers smoke in peace. Just make sure you don't light up around me because Little Miss Surgeon General is here to stay.

Kyle Therese Cranston is a Boston-based copywriter who writes fiction and creative nonfiction on the side. She is the sassy co-editor of the award-wining Mug of Woe series. Kyle also currently writes the Boston Online Dating column for Examiner.com, and her work has been featured in Chicken Soup for the Soul. Besides writing and working on trying to get her first novel published, Kyle likes to spend her time watching funny movies, dork dancing, drinking wine, eating chocolate, and making people laugh with her tales of woe.

Smoke Free Movies?
Karen Webb

What's more harmful – a four letter word or a
smoke? An organization called Smoke Free Movies
asked the Motion Picture Association of America
(MPAA) to establish an "R" rating for smoking in an
effort to cut the amount of smoking kids see in the
movies by at least half, with the aim to sharply
reduce the U.S. film industry's usefulness to Big
Tobacco's domestic and global marketing. They
claim the effect of movie smoking is clear and direct:
the more kids see, the more likely they are to start
smoking. Other studies have shown that after a
decline in the 1970s and 1980s, the amount of
smoking in American movies began to rise
dramatically in 1991, and now exceeds the amount
present in 1960. Smoke Free Movies claim that
smoking appeared in 77% of movies rated PG-13
over the past five years. Their research has
indicated that an "R" rating would prevent almost

300,000 adolescents from starting to smoke every year.

In 1953, my mother was seventeen and a junior at Mission Church High School in Roxbury. Her life revolved around school, going to Mass, swooning over Julius La Rosa and her circle of friends. She yearned to fit in and not be singled out. The fact that my mother started smoking was not the result of the many challenging situations she faced in her life. Although each separately would have been enough reason for her to pick up a pack and gave her the excuse why she couldn't quit, she started smoking to be glamorous.

From a poor family, the third of four children and the youngest daughter of a devout French Canadian Catholic mother and an Irish Catholic, sometimes abusive, father who liked his drink a bit too much, most of the money she earned babysitting was handed over to her mother to buy food or pay the rent. Occasionally, she saved enough to buy a ticket to the movie house to see the latest Bing Crosby or Frank Sinatra movie.

It was in those movies that my mother saw how Hollywood portrayed the glamorous female. She saw starlet after starlet smoking cigarettes. Bette Davis. Joan Crawford. Deborah Kerr. Grace Kelly. When she saw Arthur Godfrey, Audie Murphy, or the Texaco theatre on television at a friend's house or through a store window, she saw the ads from Brown & Williamson and Benson & Hedges. Her favorite television actress, Lucille Ball, endorsed king-sized Philip Morris cigarettes. Cigarette brands were named after the most popular political figures -- "Stevensons" and "Eisenhowers". Her favorite magazines showed pretty models holding a tiparillo or puffing a cigarette while holding a cocktail. She was bombarded with the many images and negligent seduction that helped turn America into a society of smokers. She felt young, sexy, and sophisticated like a Hollywood starlet. At an impressionable seventeen, everything she saw that showed her the perception of glamour involved a cigarette, and the seduction was too hard to resist.

At thirty six, my mother had her first heart attack. The cigarettes, nicotine and tar that had been building up in her system had started to block her arteries and the damage was starting to set in. She continued to smoke. By the time she was fifty five, she needed open heart surgery and a heart valve replaced. She continued to smoke. Two years later, the doctors found a lump in her thyroid and then a spot on her lung. The lump in her thyroid was benign. The spot on the lung wasn't, and a third of her right lung was removed. She continued to smoke. She developed spinal stenosis, where the arteries leading to her spinal column became occluded and caused tremendous pain and made it difficult to walk. She continued to smoke. Shortly thereafter, she developed emphysema and was put on oxygen. And she continued to smoke.

Over the course of forty eight years, my mother's relationship with smoking changed. From something mischievous which made her feel alive and sophisticated and one of the crowd, her smoking became her life-long crutch, what she relied on to get through life's tests. It left her feeling alone, sick, angry and embarrassed to admit she wasn't strong enough to quit. She stopped feeling glamorous somewhere along the path.

My mother had only one wish before she died. She wished for more time. Time to hold the baby I carried inside me. Time to see her grandchildren grow. Time to impart her wisdom and life experiences. My one wish was that my mother had never seen the glamour in smoking. Perhaps a rating system that included smoking would have stopped her from taking the first puff.

The MPAA claims that it created the rating system to help parents protect their children, but they do not include the use of tobacco as something they feel they need to deal with. I applaud Smoke Free Movies for taking a stance and suggesting that the MPAA rating board, as they did for movies with explicit language, adopt the "R" rating for movies that portray smoking. Four letter words, to my knowledge, have never killed millions.

Karen Webb owns a small film production firm, Pinch Hit Productions, and also owns Pinch Hit Marketing, which provides strategic marketing consulting to Fortune 500 companies. Karen is a graduate of the screenwriting program at Emerson College, has a BSBA from Lesley University, an MBA from the Babson Graduate School of Business, with post graduate studies at MIT, Harvard, and Babson. Her personal essays have been published in newspapers, magazines, and online communities such as "Moms Who Need Wine" and Will Farrell's "Funny or Die."

Butt Out
Jenn Dlugos

I have a friend who collects ashtrays. It started not from necessity but from fascination. As she wistfully remembers, it was only decades ago that ashtrays were as common in homes as flower vases, and many were just as ornate. Many of her antique ashtrays are pieces of art despite being little more than glorified trash cans. We have had many discussions about the radical shift in attitude toward smoking in our culture. A habit that was once a social staple now carries a social stigma. Even though she has long stopped being a regular smoker, her collection of unique ashtrays persists.

Ashtrays are not a common sight in souvenir shops these days, but I still always keep a lookout for a unique one for her when I travel. My personal favorite was the one a co-worker and I bought for her birthday. eBay is my go-to source for unique items. A week before her birthday, my co-worker and I held extensive email debates on the pros and cons of two different ashtrays up for auction—one in the shape of a dolphin and the other in the shape of a toilet. It was a close debate, but the dolphin eventually won out when we learned its blowhole was also a lighter.

Another memorable ashtray encounter occurred in Florida. I was on my annual Get-the-Hell-Away-From-the-Snow vacation with my mother. My mother is physically unable to walk by a gift shop of any nature without poking her head in. I'm pretty sure it's an involuntary gravitational pull. As Mom was in a Christmas store debating the pros and cons of owning a miniature nativity scene made of wooden costumed black bears, I ducked into a Mexican market with the primary objective of procuring a tequila-laden beverage. On my way to the watering hole, I spotted a little stand selling sombrero-shaped ashtrays. That is certainly not an ashtray one sees every day, so I picked up one and headed to the checkout line.

The woman in front of me in line was the curious sort, checking out what everyone else in the line was buying. When she saw my miniature sombrero ashtray, her face erupted in a smile.

"Isn't that darling!" she uttered.

I'm pretty sure no one in the history of smoking has ever referred to an ashtray as darling, but I smiled and said, "Yeah. I never saw one like this before."

"What is it? Just a decoration?"

"Oh, no," I smiled. "It's an ashtray."

Being a horror fan, I have always enjoyed Dr. Jekyll and Mr. Hyde. However, I never truly appreciated the sheer terror of watching a person transform from good to evil right before your eyes until that moment. In a split second, the kindly face of this middle-aged lady disappeared and was replaced by a look of absolute disgust.

"I'll never understand how you young people can start smoking knowing what we now know."

I honestly didn't know whether to be more upset by her self-righteousness or thrilled that I was still in the category of "young people." I'm not one who is baited easily into an emotional outburst, so I just smiled and explained that I was buying it for a friend who collects ashtrays.

"That's an awful idea," she continued. "It's just enabling her to make bad habits."

Standing in this Ode to Mexico village, I came to a full realization of the social stigma of smoking. I have witnessed smokers being shunned of course, but as a non-smoker I have never encountered this hostility head on. I've never been one to wear my non-smoking patch on my sleeve, but after this incident I had even less of an understanding of what scorning a complete stranger in public was meant to accomplish. Shaming someone has never been a way to entice them to a healthier lifestyle. It's probably just going to entice them to give you an obscene gesture on their way to their smoke break. It really just gives the shamer an opportunity to feel superior to someone for a few moments, even if it's a glaring "person in a glass house" scenario. And that is the irony of this story. While this middle-aged Public Service Announcement was scorning me for enabling bad habits that were completely contrived in her head, she was carrying a reusable grocery bag on her shoulder stuffed with enough soda, junk food, and candy to give her an irregular heartbeat.

The lady stepped up to the cashier, so I never did respond to her. Mom also walked up to me, so I passed on giving a snarky reply as she walked away. It was probably for the best, as it most definitely would have fallen under the "unladylike" category. In retrospect, I should have thanked her. She made me more conscious of how I give advice, both to smokers and just in general. There is nothing wrong with being passionate and vocal against something, but as we've learned from political postings on Facebook, an angry rant is not going to change anyone's opinion or behavior. Make your opinion known, let your loved ones know you are worried, but your advice should always come from concern and respect for the smoker. If you're only being vocal to get on your high horse and scorn, do your fellow smoker a favor...just butt out.

When the pack of cigarettes she bought on her 18th birthday went stale in her purse, Jenn Dlugos knew she was not going to be a smoker and returned to her previous vices of lottery scratch tickets and Reese's products. She is an award-winning screenwriter and is a semi-finalist in the Lifetime Television Unscripted Development Pipeline. Jenn is the co-editor of the award-winning "Woe" humor book series, including Mug of Woe: Tales to Realize Your Life is Awesome and Woe of the Road: Tales To Make You Never Want to Leave Your House. All of the Woe books are available on Amazon and Kindle. You can stalk her on her website thescriptscribe.com or on Twitter @jenndlugos.

About the Editor

Lizzy Miles changes her mind frequently about her career identity, but has always held true to her enthusiasm for written and oral storytelling. Lizzy considers herself a non-smoker at home but still smokes while in Las Vegas. She lives in Central Ohio with her husband and two cats.

Other books by Lizzy Miles

Somewhere In Between: The Hokey Pokey, Chocolate Cake and the Shared Death Experience.

The Downside of Dream Jobs: Las Vegas Performer

The Downside of Dream Jobs: Sportscaster

The Downside of Dream Jobs: Upset Recovery Flight Instructor

The Downside of Dream Jobs: Video Game Tester